ONTARIO
WILDFLOWERS

Linda Kershaw

101 Wayside Flowers

LONE
PINE

Lone Pine Publishing

The Publisher: Lone Pine Publishing
10145 – 81 Avenue
Edmonton, AB, Canada T6E 1W9

Website: www.lonepinepublishing.com

National Library of Canada Cataloguing in Publication Data

Kershaw, Linda J., 1951–
  Ontario wildflowers

Includes bibliographical references and index.
  ISBN 1-55105-285-7

  1. Wild flowers—Ontario—Identification. I. Title.
QK203.O5K477 2002   582.13'09713   C2002-910310-X

Editorial Director: Nancy Foulds
Project Editor: Dawn Loewen
Illustrations Coordinator: Carol Woo
Production Coordinator: Jennifer Fafard
Book Design, Layout & Production: Heather Markham
Production Support: Jeff Fedorkiw, Tina Tomljenovic
Cover Design: Rod Michalchuk
Scanning, Separations & Film: Elite Lithographers Co.

Cover photo: Trillium by Chris Cheadle/First Light.ca

All other photos: Linda Kershaw

DISCLAIMER: This book includes information about the historical uses of plants, but it is not meant to be a 'how-to' reference for consuming wild plants or using them for medicine. We do not recommend experimentation by readers, and we caution that many plants, including some traditional medicines, are poisonous or otherwise harmful.

We acknowledge the financial support of the Government of Canada through the Book Publishing Industry Development Program (BPIDP) for our publishing activities.

PC: P4

Contents

Colour Guide to the Flowers

The wildflowers in this guide, arranged by flower colour

orange daylily
p. 98

wood lily
p. 97

orange hawkweed
p. 64

spotted touch-me-not
p. 38

black-eyed Susan
p. 70

bird's-foot trefoil
p. 45

yellow lady's-slipper
p. 32

yellow pond-lily
p. 102

elecampane
p. 69

hairy cat's-ear
p. 62

common dandelion
p. 66

perennial sow-thistle
p. 65

common tansy
p. 74

yellow hawkweed
p. 63

annual sunflower
p. 68

Canada goldenrod
p. 75

yellow marsh-marigold
p. 103

common silverweed
p. 109

common St. John's-wort
p. 116

meadow buttercup
p. 104

fringed yellow-loosestrife
p. 122

sweet-clover
p. 46

wild parsnip
p. 83

leafy spurge
p. 81

wild mustard
p. 106

tumbleweed mustard
p. 107

butter-and-eggs
p. 34

common goat's-beard
p. 67

prickly lettuce
p. 61

common evening-
primrose, p. 120

great mullein
p. 121

sulphur cinquefoil
p. 108

pineapple-weed
p. 73

curly dock
p. 89

white death-camas
p. 95

tall meadowrue
p. 90

northern bedstraw
p. 87

common cow-parsnip
p. 84

English plantain
p. 51

spotted water-hemlock
p. 86

common water-parsnip
p. 85

common yarrow
p. 76

pearly everlasting
p. 77

Queen Anne's lace
p. 82

hoary alyssum
p. 88

buckbean
p. 92

scentless chamomile
p. 72

oxeye daisy
p. 71

snow trillium
p. 96

white water-lily
p. 101

wapato
p. 93

starry false
Solomon's-seal, p. 94

Virginia strawberry
p. 110

Canada anemone
p. 105

bunchberry
p. 111

hedge false-bindweed
p. 132

tall blue lettuce
p. 60

Canada thistle
p. 54

bladder campion
p. 115

catnip
p. 37

alsike clover
p. 49

spotted knapweed
p. 57

common milkweed
p. 123

spotted Joe-Pye weed
p. 80

lesser burdock
p. 53

spreading dogbane
p. 126

field bindweed
p. 131

swamp milkweed
p. 124

bigleaf lupine
p. 43

purple crown-vetch
p. 44

rabbitfoot clover
p. 48

pink corydalis
p. 33

red clover
p. 50

wild bergamot
p. 35

common fireweed
p. 118

brown knapweed
p. 58

nodding plumeless-
thistle, p. 56

bull thistle
p. 55

perennial sweet pea
p. 41

hairy willowherb
p. 119

musk mallow
p. 113

bouncing Bet
p. 114

purple loosestrife
p. 117

common teasel
p. 52

Philadelphia fleabane
p. 79

fringed aster
p. 78

alfalfa
p. 47

bird vetch
p. 42

beach pea
p. 40

selfheal
p. 36

creeping bellflower
p. 129

swamp vervain
p. 127

bittersweet nightshade
p. 125

northern blue flag
p. 99

early blue violet
p. 39

pickerelweed
p. 91

common viper's bugloss
p. 128

common blue-eyed-
grass, p. 100

chicory
p. 59

harebell
p. 130

cultivated flax
p. 112

Why Learn More About Wildflowers?

Imagine a summer without wildflowers: an endless monotony of brown, grey and green. Instead of that boring scene, our eyes are treated to a colourful patchwork of yellows, oranges, pinks, whites and purples that changes throughout the summer. Wildflowers add beauty and variety to the endless kilometres of roads, streets, sidewalks and pathways that crisscross our countryside.

But common wildflowers provide much more than simple decoration. Many of these hardy plants are important to the ecology of disturbed areas, such as roadsides and vacant lots. At first, newly cleared areas are simply bare soil, usually with lots of rocks, low fertility and a tendency to wash away in the rain. Only the toughest plants can survive under such harsh conditions. Those that do survive help make the soil more fertile for other plants and help hold the soil so that it isn't swept away by wind and water. Common wildflowers also provide food and shelter for many different animals.

Many wildflowers have fascinating histories that extend back for centuries. Local Native peoples used many of these plants for food and medicine long before settlers arrived from Europe. More than half of the plants in this guide, however, were brought to North America from Europe and Asia. Some arrived as valued garden plants, but others sneaked in with livestock and contaminated seed. Nowadays, a number of the species in this guide are considered weeds, unwanted but highly successful plants that can choke out crops and gardens. Still, to the casual passerby, they remain beautiful wildflowers, blanketing waysides with a mosaic of colours and textures.

It's fun to get to know wildflowers by name. Just as recognizing your friends Judy, Roy and Inger means much more than seeing a group of strangers, recognizing Queen Anne's lace, chicory and bird's-foot trefoil means more than simply seeing some plants. Once you know what to look for, it's easy to see the differences between wildflowers and to learn their names. Getting to know common flowers gives us a glimpse of the great variety of life around us, even in roadside ditches.

chicory

What Is a Wildflower?

Most of us enjoy all sorts of flowers through the year and recognize many different types, from tulips in our gardens, to carnations at the florist's, to dandelions growing wild. But what exactly is a flower, and why do plants produce such an amazing array of showy, colourful blooms?

The main function of a flower is to produce seed so that the plant can leave offspring, spread to new areas and increase in number. Technically, a flower is a shortened shoot with a compact cluster of leaves that have been modified into specialized structures (such as petals) for reproduction. Most of the wildflowers in this guide have *perfect* flowers, with both male and female parts, but some species have male flowers on one plant and female flowers on another. The illustration on this page shows a cross-section of a typical perfect flower.

Let's start with the most important parts: the male and female structures.

The male part of the typical flower is the *stamen*. Often a flower has many stamens, each consisting of a slender stalk called a *filament* tipped with a round to oblong body called an *anther*. The anther contains many tiny grains of pollen, which usually look like yellow powder. Each microscopic grain contains a sperm cell that carries half the plant's genes.

The female part of the flower is the *pistil*. Often a flower has just one pistil, but it may have many, and they may be fused. Each pistil has three main parts: the *stigma* at the tip, designed to catch pollen grains; the stalk or *style* in the middle; and the *ovary* at the base. The ovary contains one to many *ovules*, each with an egg cell that carries half the plant's genes. An ovule becomes a *seed* when its egg cell is fertilized by a sperm cell. At the same time, the ovary surrounding the seed or seeds matures into a *fruit*. Fruits come in many forms, including fleshy berries, hard nuts and pea-like pods.

The nonsexual parts of a flower help ensure successful *pollination*, which is the transfer of pollen from an anther to a stigma. A typical flower has two rings of structures surrounding its male and female parts. The outermost structure, the *calyx*, is made up of separate or fused *sepals*, which are usually green and

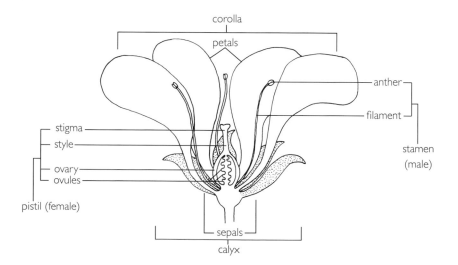

leaf-like. Sepals typically cover developing flower buds, but they may also shelter mature flower parts and eventually protect the seeds. Within the calyx is the *corolla,* which is made up of separate or fused *petals.* Most of the showy, colourful structures that we see in wildflowers are petals.

Petals help protect the stamens and pistils, but their main function is to attract pollinators. A pollinator is an animal, usually an insect, that picks up pollen and carries it to a stigma. Petals aid pollination by catching the eye of potential pollinators, by providing landing platforms for flying visitors and by discouraging visits from insects that can't pollinate the flower. Many flowers also attract pollinators by giving off a strong, sweet fragrance and by producing pools of a sugary liquid called *nectar.* You'll be amazed at the great variety of colours and forms among common wildflowers, and at the intricate ways that pollinators and flowers depend on one another.

Tips for Identifying Wildflowers

common blue-eyed-grass

1. *Stop and take a closer look.* Each wildflower has its own distinctive character. It's easy to miss important features if you can't see the details. Examine the main parts of the flower or flower cluster. How big is it? How many petals does it have? Looking closely at a plant will help you with tips 2, 3, 4 and 5.

2. *Decide which flower group your plant belongs to (pp. 16–17).* Then, page through the corresponding section of the book until you find a plant like yours

3. *Check the colour guide to the flowers (pp. 4–8).* This handy section shows photos of all 101 plants side by side for quick comparison. Flower colour can vary, so be sure to check the written description for possible variations if the picture doesn't seem quite right.

4. *Try the illustrated wildflower key (pp. 24–31).* Using a key is easy, once you get used to it. It is often a more precise way to identify a plant than a photo. If the key doesn't lead you to your plant, it will at least narrow your choices.

5. *Check other books.* This guide includes 101 common wildflowers, but hundreds of others also grow in Ontario. Many of these other species are close relatives of plants in this guide and look very similar. Even if this guide does not have the exact flower that you are trying to identify, it should give you an idea of the plant group (genus or family) to which it belongs. A list of reference books may be found on p. 138.

6. *Don't hesitate to ask.* Local naturalists and gardeners are often happy to help you identify wildflowers, and they can usually tell you stories about these fascinating plants.

To Pick or Not to Pick?

Wildflower lovers are often faced with an important question: To pick or not to pick? It is wonderful to take home a bouquet of fresh flowers and it's fun to press flowers for crafts or collections, but it would be wrong to strip our meadows and waysides of their beautiful blooms, leaving none for others to enjoy.

Most wildflowers that grow in open fields and on barren ground are hardy plants, capable of surviving and even thriving under extremely difficult conditions. Some, however, are more sensitive than you might think. For example, when you pick a wood lily, you take the leaves, stalk and all, and the plant dies. Introduced wildflowers tend to be weedier and less sensitive to cutting than native species. Often, introduced plants have adapted to a wide range of habitats and have very few natural enemies in their new home. The diseases and insects that preyed on them in Europe or Asia have usually been left behind. As a result, introduced weeds often spread rapidly, severely damaging both crops and natural vegetation as their populations expand. These flowers can, and often should, be picked.

Some common wildflowers are considered harmful to people or property and have been classified as noxious or nuisance weeds. These plants are regulated by the Ontario Weed Act, the Canada Weed Control Act and the Canada Seeds Act. The legislation requires many such weeds to be destroyed if they grow close to land that is used for agriculture or horticulture or if they somehow interfere with such uses. The table on the next page lists the wildflowers in this guide that are considered noxious or nuisance weeds.

Weedy species—especially those introduced from Eurasia—can usually be collected with little concern about quantities, and noxious weeds can be gathered freely if they are not poisonous or otherwise dangerous. On the other hand, many native wildflowers grow in sensitive habitats or are easily killed by

nodding plumeless-thistle

picking. These species should not be picked at all. Still other plants should be gathered only in moderation; for example, take just one flower in 20. This guide helps you decide whether to pick a wildflower by providing a picking category for each plant (see p. 21).

If you pick an introduced wildflower, and especially one listed in the table on this page, avoid spreading its seeds. It's also best not to plant weedy introduced species in your garden, in case they spread to natural areas and create problems.

Always treat native plants with respect, and take only as much as you need. If you just want to press the flowers, take only the flowers and leave the rest of the plant to grow.

Noxious and Nuisance Weeds in This Guide

COMMON NAME	SCIENTIFIC NAME	PAGE NUMBER
poison-ivy	*Toxicodendron radicans*	15
butter-and-eggs	*Linaria vulgaris*	34
English plantain	*Plantago lanceolata*	51
Canada thistle	*Cirsium arvense*	54
bull thistle	*Cirsium vulgare*	55
nodding plumeless-thistle	*Carduus nutans*	56
spotted knapweed	*Centaurea biebersteinii*	57
brown knapweed	*Centaurea jacea*	58
chicory	*Cichorium intybus*	59
perennial sow-thistle	*Sonchus arvensis*	65
common dandelion	*Taraxacum officinale*	66
common goat's-beard	*Tragopogon dubius*	67
oxeye daisy	*Leucanthemum vulgare*	71
scentless chamomile	*Tripleurospermum perforata*	72
stinking chamomile	*Anthemis cotula*	72
common tansy	*Tanacetum vulgare*	74
leafy spurge	*Euphorbia esula*	81
Queen Anne's lace	*Daucus carota*	82
spotted water-hemlock	*Cicuta maculata*	86
curly dock	*Rumex crispus*	89
white death-camas	*Zigadenus elegans*	95
meadow buttercup	*Ranunculus acris*	104
wild mustard	*Sinapis arvensis*	106
bouncing Bet	*Saponaria officinalis*	114
bladder campion	*Silene vulgaris*	115
purple loosestrife	*Lythrum salicaria*	117
common milkweed	*Asclepias syriaca*	123
spreading dogbane	*Apocynum androsaemifolium*	126
common viper's bugloss	*Echium vulgare*	128
creeping bellflower	*Campanula rapunculoides*	129
field bindweed	*Convolvulus arvensis*	131
hedge false-bindweed	*Calystegia sepium*	132

Danger, Beware!

A beautiful patch of wildflowers may demand a closer look, but before you rush over to investigate, take time to look around for possible dangers. Ditches often harbour broken glass and sharp sticks. Sudden drops may lie hidden under dense growth of vines and grasses. When soil is bare, slopes can be unstable (especially when they're wet) and may start to slide from under you.

If you are looking at flowers near a road, remember to watch for passing vehicles. It's also unwise to use roadside plants for food or medicine. Plants growing along roads are usually exposed to many different pollutants. Vehicle exhaust and dust settle on plants; runoff from the road carries salt, oil and other pollutants to nearby soil; and pest-control programs can coat plants with herbicides and insecticides. All in all, it's safer and more enjoyable to study plants well away from heavy traffic.

Even in pristine areas, proceed with caution if you are using *any* plant for food or medicine. Poisonous plants can be confused with edible species. The carrot family (pp. 82–86) is especially dangerous. Some of our most poisonous plants (poison-hemlock and spotted water-hemlock, p. 86) are very similar to edible plants such as wild parsnip (p. 83) and Queen Anne's lace (p. 82). Carelessly consuming plants in the carrot family is a sort of herbal Russian roulette. Never eat any part of a plant unless you are 100% sure of its identity.

Even with good identification, there can be problems. One person may be allergic to a berry that someone else eats all the time. People with special health considerations such as pregnancy or heart problems may be harmed by a plant that others can use safely.

spotted water-hemlock

Potentially harmful wildflowers are identified as such in this book. However, two other plants that commonly harm people do not have showy flowers; their inconspicuousness, in fact, makes them even more dangerous. Both can make your skin burn and itch. It's important to learn to recognize these plants:

Stinging nettle *(Urtica dioica)*. With its inconspicuous clusters of tiny, green to purplish flowers, stinging nettle blends in easily with other plants. It can usually be found in low meadows, ditches, gullies and other places where soils are rich and moist. The four-sided stems reach 1–3 m in height, much taller than most of the mint species with which this plant could be confused. Stinging nettle can be recognized by its opposite, slender-stalked leaves, which have coarsely toothed, lance-shaped to heart-shaped blades 4–15 cm long, and of course by its tiny stinging hairs if you are unfortunate enough to touch the plant. Each hollow hair has a swollen base that contains a droplet of formic acid, the same chemical that gives attacking ants their sting.

When the hair pierces you, it injects the acid into your skin, causing itching or burning that lasts anywhere from a few minutes to a couple of days. Usually the effect lasts for less than an hour, but it can be very irritating. Don't panic. It should soon go away. Some say that rubbing the sting with the roots of the offending plant helps to reduce the burning, but this cure may be more psychological than physical.

Poison-ivy *(Toxicodendron radicans)*. Poison ivy is a highly variable plant, ranging from a bushy herb 10–15 cm tall to a large, woody vine a few metres long. It can grow anywhere from open, sandy ridges to moist, shady nooks, and it often grows in colonies that cover the ground. In autumn, the leaves may turn bright red, and white, berry-like fruits may be seen. Poison-ivy is usually recognized by its glossy green leaves that are divided into three pointed, 5–10 cm long leaflets with smooth or slightly toothed edges. If you're not sure whether a plant is poison-ivy, just remember the rhyme 'Leaves of three, let it be.'

This inconspicuous plant leaves deposits of irritating resin on any-

stinging nettle (above), poison-ivy (below)

thing it contacts. The resin can be removed by washing with strong soap and water, but if it is left on skin more than 5–10 minutes, it usually causes a rash. Pets, tools, clothing and even smoke from burning poison-ivy plants can carry the harmful substance (an allergen) to unsuspecting victims. Once the rash appears, ointments and antihistamines can help reduce itching and swelling. Traditional treatments included applying dried blood or the sap from touch-me-not or stinging nettle. Sensitivity varies from one person to the next, and bad cases may require a visit to the doctor.

Organization of the Guide

This guide includes 101 wildflowers common along Ontario waysides and in pastures, orchards and abandoned lots. Almost all are conspicuous even to highway travellers. A few less noticeable species (e.g., Virginia strawberry) are also included because they are so common. Snow trillium is different from most of the plants because it grows in woodlands rather than in open areas; it is included because it is our provincial flower.

Two features usually help us recognize flowers: colour and structure. The wildflowers in this book are organized by colour in the guide to the flowers on pp. 4–8, but remember that flower colour can vary. For example, bouncing Bet (p. 114) may be pink at one site and white at another. Check the flower descriptions for the full range of colours.

Within the book, the wildflowers are divided into five major sections based on the structure of flowers or flower clusters:

Section 1: Two-Sided Flowers (pp. 32–47)

This section includes some of our most unusual flowers. These two-sided, or *bilaterally symmetrical*, flowers can be divided into two equal halves along only a single line. A good example of a two-sided flower is a violet.

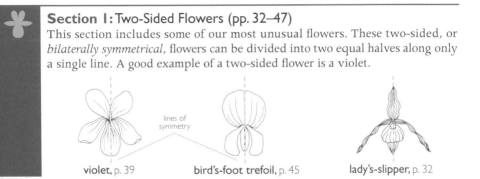

lines of symmetry

violet, p. 39   bird's-foot trefoil, p. 45   lady's-slipper, p. 32

Section 2: Tiny Stalkless Flowers in Compact Clusters (pp. 48–80)

Some plants have tiny (1–5 mm wide), apparently stalkless flowers in dense, head-like clusters. These clusters, which often appear as individual flowers, are called *flowerheads*. A daisy, for example, is a flowerhead, not a single flower.

Most wildflowers in Section 2 belong to the large and variable aster family. These plants have flowerheads ranging from single, huge sunflowers to scores of small flowerheads in goldenrods. The structure of a typical aster flowerhead is illustrated in the glossary (p. 135).

There is some overlap between sections 1 and 2, because some members of the pea family (such as clovers, pp. 48–50) have tiny, 2-sided flowers that form dense spikes and heads. These flowers are at the beginning of Section 2.

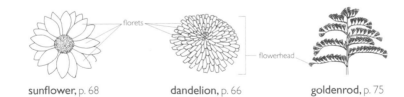

florets

flowerhead

sunflower, p. 68   dandelion, p. 66   goldenrod, p. 75

Section 3: Tiny Stalked Flowers in Branched Clusters (pp. 81–90)

Many flowers are so tiny, you may need a magnifying glass to see them clearly. Even the tiniest blooms, however, become conspicuous if there are enough of them. The individual flowers in this section are only 1–5 mm wide, but dozens or even hundreds of them combine to form showy, lacy clusters.

Queen Anne's lace, p. 82   meadowrue, p. 90   bedstraw, p. 87   dock, p. 89

Section 4: Circular Flowers with Distinct Petals (pp. 91–125)

When most people think of a flower, they think of a plant from this section. Circular, or *radially symmetrical*, flowers can be divided into two equal parts along two or more lines. The circular flowers in Section 4 are more than 5 mm across and have petals that are divided at least halfway to their bases, so they stand out clearly as individual petals. Section 4 includes a great variety of flowers, ranging from pond-lilies to milkweeds.

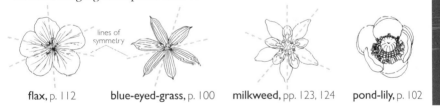

flax, p. 112   blue-eyed-grass, p. 100   milkweed, pp. 123, 124   pond-lily, p. 102

Section 5: Circular Flowers with Fused Petals (pp. 126–132)

This relatively small section includes funnel-shaped and bell-shaped flowers. These circular (radially symmetrical) flowers are more than 5 mm across and have petals that are fused for more than half their length, creating a tube-like structure tipped with the petal lobes.

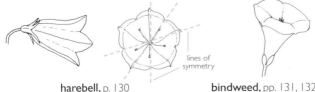

harebell, p. 130   bindweed, pp. 131, 132   dogbane, p. 126

Information for Each Species

The following information is provided for each wildflower in this guide.

COMMON AND SCIENTIFIC NAMES

Each entry begins with a common name for the wildflower. This name is widely used and generally accepted in Ontario for that particular plant.

Most plants, and especially most widespread plants like the ones in this guide, have lots of common names. Many wildflowers have long histories, so it's not unusual for a species to have 20 or more common names. Different names can evolve in different regions, at different times and in reference to different uses or stories. You may already know some of these plants by other names.

The common name is followed by the scientific (Latin) name for the species. Although scientific names may be hard to pronounce and remember at first, they are much less confusing than common names in the long run. Generally, a species has only one accepted scientific name, and this name can be changed only when research shows that the original classification was wrong or that an earlier name was overlooked. Scientific names are much less changeable than common names because they have to be presented in reputable publications and accepted by taxonomists (scientists who study classification) before they can be accepted. Publication also has the advantage of keeping a record of all of the scientific names that have ever been used for a plant, so it's possible to trace origins of names and avoid confusion. Best of all, scientific names apply all over the world, so people who speak different languages can all use the same name.

The family name is also given for each species, in the coloured header bar at the top of the page. As the word suggests, a family is a group of related plants. Knowing which family a wildflower belongs to can help you recognize its relatives. For example, once you learn the general features of peas, you can go straight to the pea family (pp. 40–50) when you see a plant with those features. Common family names also have Latin counterparts: the table on p. 140 lists the common and scientific family names along with page ranges for quick reference.

bull thistle

NOTES

Below the names, each species entry begins with some notes of interest about the wildflower. This section will vary greatly but includes the following types of information.

Natural History

Wildflowers depend on many different parts of their environment to survive and reproduce. Information about natural history could include interactions between plants and animals. For example, which animals use these plants for food or shelter? How do plants protect themselves from being eaten?

Many common flowers are successful colonizers, so some notes describe how they reproduce. Why has this wildflower succeeded where others have failed? How are its flowers pollinated to produce seed? How are its seeds carried to new sites? Can it spread in other ways? Many wildflowers have been spread around the world by human activities such as gardening, farming and shipping. Information about immigration tells when the plant arrived, where it spread and how, and whether it has become a troublesome weed.

annual sunflower

Human Uses

Wildflowers have been used by humans for centuries. A wide range of uses may be presented for a species, but it should be stressed that the reliability of the information varies greatly. Much of it comes from very old sources, and few of the uses have been studied by modern-day researchers.

Food and medicine. Many wildflowers have been important to people as food and medicine. The notes may describe where, when and how plants were collected, what parts were used and how they were processed. For example, were the plants eaten raw, pickled, steamed, boiled or fried? Were their healing properties extracted in teas, syrups or tinctures (alcohol extracts), or were plants simply applied in poultices or inhaled as smoke? Perhaps some plants required special preparation, such as removal of tough or spiny outer layers or soaking in lye to remove bitter chemicals.

Leaves, stems and buds may be added to salads, sandwiches, stews, soups, stir-fries, cakes, puddings, omelets, cheeses and teas. Some have been used to thicken gravy or flavour liqueurs. Roots are occasionally eaten raw in salads, but usually they have been cooked as a vegetable or dried and ground into flour. Some roots have been used to make wine, tea or coffee and to flavour other dishes. Edible flowers and flower pollen are usually used simply as a garnish, but starchy, oil-rich seeds have been used widely for food. Many types of seeds can be gathered and ground into meal or flour for making gruel, cakes and breads. Still others can be roasted to make coffee-like drinks.

The wildflowers in this guide have been used to treat a wide array of ailments, ranging from cuts, bruises and burns to lupus, malaria and multiple sclerosis. Some have been used cosmetically to remove warts and pimples, and many have been used to treat everyday problems such as upset stomachs, headaches, cramps and colds. Over the years, many wild plants have been applied in poultices and lotions to relieve the aches of arthritis and rheumatism. Still others have been used in medicines for treating heart disease and diabetes. Remember that very few of these wide-ranging medicinal uses have been tested scientifically.

Wild plants should be used as food or medicine only with **extreme caution**. See the 'Danger, Beware' section on p. 14 and the individual species entries for more information.

cultivated flax

Household uses. The range of uses for common plants seems to have been limited only by the imagination of industrious residents. Some of the wildflowers in this guide have been used for making soap, rubber, deodorant or insect repellent. Others have provided toilet paper, cosmetics and stuffing for mattresses and pillows. Many have been used as a source of fibre for thread, cord, twine, cloth, rope and even fishnets. The notes may describe where, when and how plants were collected, what parts were used and how they were processed.

Farming. Some plants were brought to North America as sources of animal feed or green manure. The notes for these plants may include livestock preferences, nectar production (for honey) and the importance of plants in soil improvement programs.

Landscaping. Many successful wayside wildflowers are cultivated as hardy ornamentals. Still others are planted on exposed ground to stabilize slopes and enrich soil. The notes about these plants may include advantages or disadvantages of introducing wildflowers into your garden, and the importance of some species for landscaping parks and roadsides.

Superstitions and Folklore

Many myths, legends and superstitions have become associated with wild plants. Plant lore is especially well known for Eurasian species because stories have been written down for hundreds of years in that part of the world. Some wildflowers have been used as charms against snakes, witches and other threats. Still others were chewed and rubbed onto bodies as a source of strength, energy and protection from evil forces.

Meaning of Names

Most scientific names are based on Greek or Latin words. These strange-sounding words often tell us something about the history or appearance of the plant. By understanding the name, you can learn something about the wildflower and you may find the name easier to remember. If a name has changed recently, its previous name may be included in the notes.

IDENTIFICATION POINTS

The bottom part of each species entry gives a short description of the plant, focusing on features that are important for identifying it: the plant's form and its leaves, flowers and fruits. Most of the information in this section is presented in everyday language, but sometimes more technical terms have to be used. If you don't understand a word, look in the illustrated glossary (pp. 133–137) for an easy-to-understand explanation.

Size ranges are given for most of the identifying features. A ruler is printed on the back cover for quick reference when you need to check sizes.

Blooming times are also given; knowing when a plant blooms can often help in identifying it.

HABITAT AND DISTRIBUTION

For each wildflower, you will also find information about where to look for it. This information comes in two parts. The first, 'Habitat,' describes the type of ecosystem where the wildflower usually grows. Most of the plants in this guide thrive on disturbed ground such as roadsides, but many also grow in more natural habitats such as meadows, woods, streamsides and lakeshores. 'Habitat' is followed by 'Distribution,' which describes the geographical range of the wildflower. If the species has been introduced from elsewhere in the

yellow marsh-marigold

world, its distribution begins with the region where it originated, followed by the parts of North America (north of Mexico) where it now grows wild.

PICKING GUIDELINE

At the very end of the species description, you will find a general guide to how many blooms it is acceptable to pick:

Pick none: for sensitive native wildflowers or those that grow in sensitive habitats. Don't pick these at all, and avoid trampling them.

Pick a few: for common native plants. Take a few blooms, but be sure to leave just as many behind for others to enjoy.

Pick freely: for abundant, weedy plants (mainly introduced), some of which are noxious or nuisance weeds. Take all you want!

Some of the plants in this guide may be dangerous to pick because they are poisonous or have spines, hairs, sap or pollen that can irritate skin. These species have the word *caution* in the 'Pick' part of the description. For example, the picking guideline for Canada thistle is 'freely; caution' because this plant is classified as a noxious weed but it is covered in sharp spines—take all you want, but look out for the prickles. Yellow marsh-marigold, on the other hand, is sensitive to picking and its sap can irritate sensitive skin. Its picking code is 'none; caution'—you shouldn't pick it, but you wouldn't want to, anyway, because the sap could burn your skin.

Of course, these categories apply to plants that are well established in the wild. In some regions, wildflowers are planted along highways to add beauty to barren landscapes and to stabilize and improve soils. If a roadside has been seeded recently, its young plants should be left alone to multiply.

Fun with Flowers

Wildflowers add beauty to fields and waysides, and they add interest to trips and outings. When kids are travelling, it's fun to keep track of all of the different wildflowers along the way. See who can find the first orange, red or purple wildflower, or who can spot the most species in 10 km, 10 minutes or all day.

As you get to know wildflowers, you may want to keep track of which ones you've seen. All of the species in this guide are listed in a checklist on p. 139.

It's hard to identify flowers when you're zooming along at highway speed, and it's dangerous to stop on busy roads. Take time for short walks at roadside pullouts and parks: you'll be surprised at what you discover. Better yet, follow the road less travelled. Back roads let you enjoy a relaxed pace and pull over more easily.

Closer to home, get to know the wildflowers in your neighbourhood and watch them as they grow. It's fun to keep a nature diary with notes, sketches and pressed leaves and flowers, describing how plants change through the summer and from year to year. Plants are very cooperative: they stay in the same place throughout their lifetime, and they stand still while you examine them, making them excellent subjects for drawings, paintings and photos.

Everyone enjoys bouquets of freshly cut flowers, and some wildflowers will last for days if they're treated properly. Flowers need to be put into water as soon as possible so they don't wilt. When you pick a plant, it continues to try to draw water up its stem, and air is sucked into the little tubes that carry liquid to the flower. This air can block the movement of water. Just before you put your bouquet in water, cut off the bottom few centimetres of each stem to trim off the airlock and allow water to move up the stem to nourish the flowers and leaves. Try adding food colouring to the water, and watch white flowers magically change colour.

With luck, fresh flowers can last for a week, but dried flowers remain beautiful for months or even years. Some flowers preserve better than others. For example, black-eyed Susan and young Queen Anne's lace flowers dry well, but more delicate blooms such as spotted touch-me-not and musk mallow soon fade. Fruit clusters such as the shiny brown capsules of bladder campion and prickly brown heads of teasel can also add interest to winter bouquets and wreaths.

Many common wildflowers can be dried by simply hanging them in bundles in a warm, dark, dry place. Generally, the more quickly a flower dries, the better its colour will be. If the bundles become too hot, their flowers can scorch and fade, but if they are too cool or damp they may turn brown or mould.

Another way to dry wild-flowers is to press them between sheets of absorbent paper such as newsprint. Simply lay the flower between two sheets of paper on a flat surface, put another flat surface over the paper and set a weight on top. Often people press plants in books, but this doesn't always work well; very little air gets to the plant, so the flower and leaves may mould, and the book can be damaged. For better results, make your own plant press. Simply use pieces of corrugated cardboard for your flat surfaces and alternate layers of cardboard, paper, plants, paper, cardboard and so on. When you've laid all your flowers in place, strap or tie the layers together in a snug bundle and set it in a warm place to dry. Air will pass through the tunnels in the cardboard, drying the flowers quickly so that they keep their colour. If the flowers are bulky, you may need to put a weight on top to help flatten them. If you can't get everything to lie the way you want it to, try pressing the flower for a few hours, then carefully rearrange the petals and leaves while they are still damp.

Pressed flowers are easy to store, and they can be used in many ways. A wildflower collection is a wonderful memento of a trip. Each flower can remind you of a special stop along the way. It's a good idea to write the name of each plant and the place and date you collected it on the pressing paper.

Many crafts projects can make use of pressed flowers. The flowers can be glued to paper and covered with clear plastic to make beautiful notecards and bookmarks. Pressed flowers can also be arranged on cardstock and framed behind glass. Similarly, dried wildflowers set between two sheets of glass make beautiful wall hangings, sun-catchers and decorations. Pressed clusters of Queen Anne's lace flowers look like delicate snowflakes, so they are perfect for holiday decorations.

The possibilities are endless—just use your imagination!

Using a Key to Identify Wildflowers

A quick and easy way to identify wildflowers is to use a key. Keys ask you questions about the flower you are trying to identify, and you provide the answers. Each answer leads you either to another set of choices or to the name of the wildflower. By using a key, you can narrow your possibilities without having to look through the entire book.

This is a *dichotomous* key, which simply means that the choices are in pairs so you always choose between two alternatives. For example, read **1a** and **1b**. If the flowers are tiny (1–5 mm across), **1a** is right, so you go to choice **2: 2a** or **2b**. If the flowers are larger, **1b** is correct, so you go to choice **8: 8a** or **8b**. Eventually, you should come to an illustration of your flower. Turn to the page number indicated for that flower to learn more about it.

You can sometimes arrive at the same answer in more than one way. For example, you may look at a daisy and think that it is a single flower, but someone else may know that it is really a flowerhead made up of many tiny flowers. Some of these potential problems have been taken into consideration in this key, so that you can identify the daisy either way.

If you don't understand some of the words used in the key or elsewhere in the guide, check the illustrated glossary (p. 133).

Key to the Wildflowers in This Book

Note: In this key, 'petals' refers to true petals, petal-like sepals, petal-like bracts and petal-like florets.

1a Flowers or flowerheads tiny, usually 1–5 mm across **2**

1b Flowers or flowerheads larger (over 5 mm across), single or in showy clusters **8**

2a Flowers in head-like clusters or spikes; individual flowers stalkless or stalks too short to be seen **3**

2b Flowers in looser clusters that are branched and often lacy; individual flowers or small (1–5 mm) flowerheads clearly stalked **7**

3a Flower clusters appearing to be individual flowers, made up of a dense central clump of tiny flowers surrounded by a ring of showier, petal-like flowers or bracts **4**

3b Flower clusters head-like, composed of flowers that are all similar **5**

4a Flowerheads large and showy, usually at least 2 cm across

| bunchberry p. 111 | sunflower p. 68 | black-eyed Susan p. 70 | oxeye daisy, p. 71 chamomile, p. 72 |

| aster p. 78 | fleabane p. 79 | elecampane p. 69 | brown knapweed p. 58 |

4b Flowerheads smaller, 0.5–2 cm across, but forming showy branched clusters

| goldenrod p. 75 | yarrow p. 76 | pearly everlasting p. 77 | spurge p. 81 |

5a Each tiny flower not flat and petal-like, usually pea-like or with a tube of fused petals, but often too tiny to tell **6**

5b Each tiny flower appearing to be a single petal, its true petals fused into a ribbon-like strap

| chicory p. 59 | lettuce pp. 60, 61 | cat's-ear p. 62 | hawkweed pp. 63, 64 |

| sow-thistle p. 65 | dandelion p. 66 | goat's-beard p. 67 |

6a 'Petals' expanded and showy

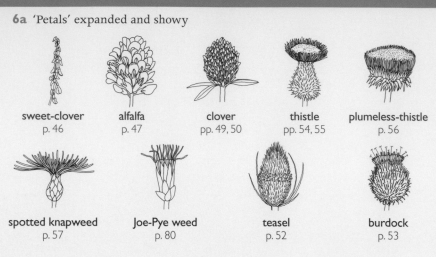

sweet-clover	alfalfa	clover	thistle	plumeless-thistle
p. 46	p. 47	pp. 49, 50	pp. 54, 55	p. 56

spotted knapweed	Joe-Pye weed	teasel	burdock
p. 57	p. 80	p. 52	p. 53

6b Petals inconspicuous, often hidden by bristles or absent altogether

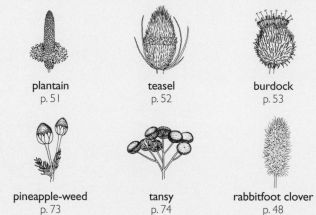

plantain	teasel	burdock
p. 51	p. 52	p. 53

pineapple-weed	tansy	rabbitfoot clover
p. 73	p. 74	p. 48

7a Flower clusters wide, with flat or rounded tops, often umbrella-shaped

yarrow	pearly everlasting	Joe-Pye weed	Queen Anne's lace
p. 76	p. 77	p. 80	p. 82

parsnip	cow-parsnip	water-parsnip	water-hemlock
p. 83	p. 84	p. 85	p. 86

7b Flower clusters more elongated, usually tapered to a point at the tip

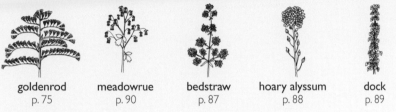

goldenrod	meadowrue	bedstraw	hoary alyssum	dock
p. 75	p. 90	p. 87	p. 88	p. 89

8a Flowers 2-sided (bilaterally symmetrical), divisible into 2 equal parts along a single line through the centre, usually with an upper and a lower lip . . . **9**

8b Flowers or flower-like heads round or star-shaped (radially symmetrical), divisible into 2 equal parts along 2 or more lines through the centre . . **10**

9a Flowers pea-like, with 5 separate petals including 1–2 upper petals, 2 side (wing) petals and a lower lip formed by 1–2 petals

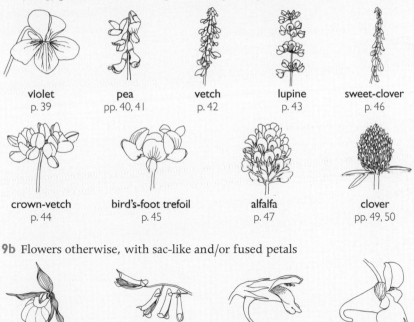

violet	pea	vetch	lupine	sweet-clover
p. 39	pp. 40, 41	p. 42	p. 43	p. 46

crown-vetch	bird's-foot trefoil	alfalfa	clover
p. 44	p. 45	p. 47	pp. 49, 50

9b Flowers otherwise, with sac-like and/or fused petals

lady's-slipper	corydalis	butter-and-eggs	touch-me-not
p. 32	p. 33	p. 34	p. 38

wild bergamot	selfheal	catnip	pickerelweed
p. 35	p. 36	p. 37	p. 91

10a 'Petals' separate for at least half their length, appearing as distinct petals **11**

10b Petals fused for more than half their length to form tubes, funnels or bells

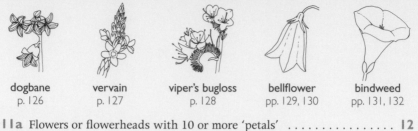

dogbane
p. 126

vervain
p. 127

viper's bugloss
p. 128

bellflower
pp. 129, 130

bindweed
pp. 131, 132

11a Flowers or flowerheads with 10 or more 'petals' **12**

11b Flowers or flowerheads with less than 10 'petals' **14**

12a Flowerheads composed of one type of 'petal' or small flower **13**

12b Flowerheads with a ring of 'petals' around a compact button of tiny tubular florets

elecampane
p. 69

fleabane
p. 79

aster
p. 78

oxeye daisy, p. 71
chamomile, p. 72

black-eyed Susan
p. 70

sunflower
p. 68

pearly everlasting
p. 77

brown knapweed
p. 58

13a 'Petals' flattened, strap-like or lance-shaped

water-lily
p. 101

hawkweed
pp. 63, 64

cat's-ear
p. 62

sow-thistle
p. 65

dandelion
p. 66

goat's-beard
p. 67

chicory
p. 59

lettuce
pp. 60, 61

13b 'Petals' (tiny flowers) tubular or pea-like

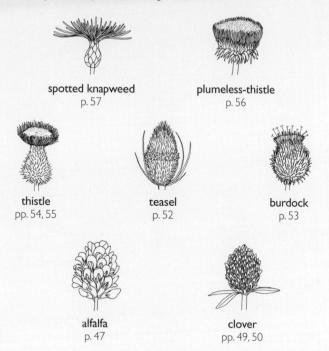

spotted knapweed
p. 57

plumeless-thistle
p. 56

thistle
pp. 54, 55

teasel
p. 52

burdock
p. 53

alfalfa
p. 47

clover
pp. 49, 50

14a Flowers with 3 or more showy 'petals' 15
14b Flowers or flowerheads with 0–2 showy 'petals'

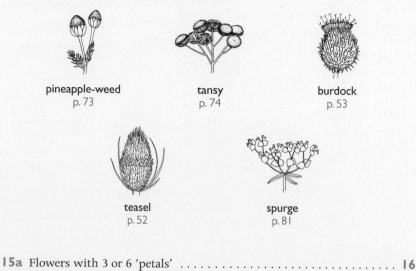

pineapple-weed
p. 73

tansy
p. 74

burdock
p. 53

teasel
p. 52

spurge
p. 81

15a Flowers with 3 or 6 'petals' 16
15b Flowers with 4 or 5 'petals' (marsh-marigold can have 5–9) 17

16a Flowers small, 0.6–3 cm across

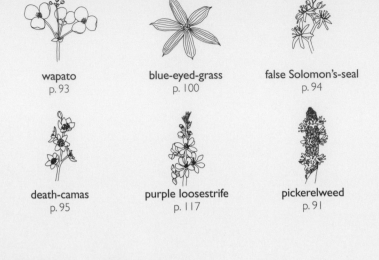

| wapato | blue-eyed-grass | false Solomon's-seal |
| p. 93 | p. 100 | p. 94 |

| death-camas | purple loosestrife | pickerelweed |
| p. 95 | p. 117 | p. 91 |

16b Flowers large, more than 3 cm across

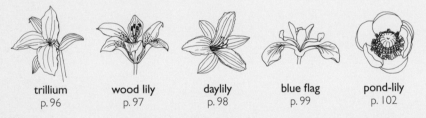

| trillium | wood lily | daylily | blue flag | pond-lily |
| p. 96 | p. 97 | p. 98 | p. 99 | p. 102 |

17a Flowers with 5 'petals' (marsh-marigold can have 5–9) **18**

17b Flowers cross-shaped, with 4 'petals'

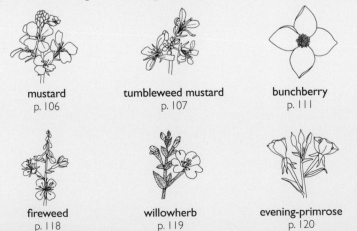

| mustard | tumbleweed mustard | bunchberry |
| p. 106 | p. 107 | p. 111 |

| fireweed | willowherb | evening-primrose |
| p. 118 | p. 119 | p. 120 |

18a Flowers and leaves alternately attached (one per joint) **19**

18b Flowers and leaves paired or whorled (2 or more per joint)

bouncing Bet
p. 114

campion
p. 115

St. John's-wort
p. 116

yellow-loosestrife
p. 122

milkweed
pp. 123, 124

19a 'Petals' yellow

marsh-marigold
p. 103

buttercup
p. 104

cinquefoil, p. 108
silverweed, p. 109

mullein
p. 121

19b 'Petals' white, pink, red or purple

anemone
p. 105

strawberry
p. 110

flax
p. 112

mallow
p. 113

buckbean
p. 92

nightshade
p. 125

Yellow Lady's-Slipper
Cypripedium parviflorum

This beautiful orchid is widespread but never common, so it is always an exciting discovery. You may be tempted to transplant lady's-slippers to your garden, but please leave them for others to enjoy. Orchid roots grow with special fungi (mycorrhizae) that help them take nutrients from the soil. If the orchid's specific fungus doesn't grow in your garden, neither can the orchid. • The unusual flowers are designed to trap insects. Bees and flies enter easily through the mouth of the slipper, but once inside they slide down smooth, steep walls. Eventually, they discover a hairy strip and follow it out, but along the way they must first hit the stigma (female part) and then pick up a sticky clump of pollen from the male part. • This species has also been called *C. calceolus*.

Plant: erect perennial 20–80 cm tall, from fibrous roots **Leaves:** oval to lance-shaped, 6–20 cm long, with sheathing bases **Flowers:** with 4 (3 separate, 2 fused) purplish brown to greenish yellow, 3–8 cm tepals around a yellow, 2–5 cm, pouched lip; 1–2 flowers per stalk **Blooms:** May to July **Fruits:** oblong capsules containing some 15,000 seeds **Habitat:** moist roadsides and woodlands **Distribution:** native across North America and around the world **Pick:** none

Pink Corydalis
Corydalis sempervirens

Slender, delicate pink corydalis often seems to appear out of nowhere in recently disturbed or burned areas. Insects in search of nectar must be strong enough to force the mouth of the flower open and must have tongues long enough to reach the nectar at the base of the flower tube. Frustrated short-tongued bees often chew small holes through the spur to steal nectar. Robbed flowers will not be pollinated, so they cannot produce seed. In Europe, some *Corydalis* species are believed to be headed for extinction because of intensive bee burglary. • Some *Corydalis* species have sedative and pain-killing compounds, but many also contain toxic alkaloids.

Plant: bluish green perennial 20–80 cm tall **Leaves:** twice pinnately divided into 1–3 cm long, mostly 3-lobed leaflets **Flowers:** tubular, rose to purplish, with a yellow tip and a small pouch (spur) at the base, 1–1.7 cm long; dangling in small, pyramid-shaped clusters **Blooms:** May to September **Fruits:** slender, cylindrical pods, containing and constricted between shiny black, finely bumpy, 1 mm seeds **Habitat:** dry, often rocky clearings **Distribution:** native from Newfoundland to Alaska, south through the eastern U.S. **Pick:** a few

Butter-and-Eggs
Linaria vulgaris

Butter-and-eggs is a native of Asia and became popular in Europe as a hardy ornamental that added lots of colour and needed little care. It was also successful on our continent, where it spread rapidly by seed (up to 8700 per plant) and by creeping underground stems. • Its acrid juice makes butter-and-eggs distasteful to animals and potentially poisonous to humans. In Scandinavia, the plants were boiled in milk to make an insecticide used for attracting and poisoning flies. • Only large insects such as honeybees and hawk moths are strong enough to open the lips of these flowers and have tongues long enough to reach the nectar. If you hold a flower up to the light, you can see the nectar in its spur. • This plant is sometimes called toadflax.

Plant: erect, grey-green perennial 30–80 cm tall, from creeping roots **Leaves:** many, alternate (lower leaves sometimes paired), slender, tapered to a stalk-like base, 2–6 cm long **Flowers:** snapdragon-like, 2–3.5 cm long, yellow with an orange lower lip and a slender, yellow, backward-pointing tube (spur); many borne in compact spikes **Blooms:** May to September **Fruits:** rounded, 8–12 mm capsules containing winged seeds **Habitat:** dry, disturbed ground **Distribution:** Eurasia; naturalized from Newfoundland to Alaska to Texas **Pick:** freely

Wild Bergamot
Monarda fistulosa

European settlers and Native peoples used this aromatic plant for flavouring salads, cooked vegetables and stews and for making a pleasant minty tea. Dried, powdered leaves were sprinkled on food to keep flies and other insects away and were rubbed onto hair, skin, clothing and even favourite horses as perfume. The plant's fragrance was likened to that of bergamot (the citrus used to flavour Earl Grey tea), giving rise to the name wild bergamot. Settlers soon began planting this beautiful, useful herb and introduced it to England in 1744 as an edible ornamental and tea flavouring. Since then, many hybrids have been developed, providing a variety of long-lasting, rose pink to deep red blooms for bouquets of cut flowers. Wild bergamot will attract butterflies and hummingbirds to the garden. It is best grown from seed.

Plant: grey-green, square-stemmed perennial, 50–120 cm tall, from spreading rootstock
Leaves: paired, lance-shaped, toothed, stalked, 6–10 cm long, smaller upwards
Flowers: lavender to purple or yellowish pink, 2–3.5 cm long, tubular, with a 3-lobed lower lip and a slender, fuzzy, 2-lobed upper lip tipped with 2 projecting stamens; flowers in head-like clusters **Blooms:** June to September **Fruits:** 4 small nutlets
Habitat: upland wooded and open sites
Distribution: native from Quebec to B.C. to the southern U.S. **Pick:** a few

Selfheal

Prunella vulgaris

I mpressive common names, such as selfheal and healall, suggest that this inconspicuous weed has a remarkable history in medicine. Unfortunately, that is not the case. Like many herbs, selfheal was added to all-purpose salves, washes, gargles and syrups, and it was used to make medicinal teas for fevers and digestive upsets, but it seems to have been seldom used. Because the small flowers were likened to open mouths, 17th-century healers believed it would cure mouth and throat infections. • Today, selfheal is known mainly as a common weed and lawn pest that blooms when only 5 cm tall. The plant can be eaten raw or cooked or used to make a flavourful tea, so harvesting it is an environmentally friendly way to control its spread.

Plant: clumped perennial with 4-sided stems 10–30 cm tall **Leaves:** paired, 2–9 cm long, stalked **Flowers:** purplish blue (sometimes pink to white), 1–2 cm long, tubular, with a hooded upper lip and broad, 3-lobed lower lip; borne in the axils of reddish-fringed bracts in dense, 2–5 cm long spikes **Blooms:** May to September **Fruits:** 4 smooth nutlets, 2 mm long **Habitat:** moist, disturbed sites **Distribution:** native and partly introduced from Newfoundland to B.C., Alaska and Texas **Pick:** freely

Catnip
Nepeta cataria

Catnip is best known for the play-ful behaviour it produces in many cats, from house cats to lions and jaguars. Frenzied felines often destroy catnip plants with their antics. Cats are attracted to the fragrance given off by bruised or wilted foliage, hence the old saying 'If you set it, cats will eat it; if you sow it, cats don't know it.' Although its effects on humans are much less notable, people have used catnip for centuries as a seasoning and medicine. Catnip tea has a lemony-minty flavour and has been taken to soothe digestive upsets, calm jangled nerves and relieve coughs, colds and cramps. The leaves have also been smoked to relieve bronchitis. Though these uses have not been proven to be efficacious, catnip is pleasant-flavoured and safe to use in moderation. • The name *Nepeta* may be a reference to the Roman town Nepeti, where catnip was said to grow abundantly.

Plant: greyish-downy perennial 30–100 cm tall, from taproot **Leaves:** paired, heart-shaped to triangular, 3–8 cm long, coarsely toothed, blades twice as long as stalks **Flowers:** white or pale lavender with pink or purple dots, 2-lipped, funnel-shaped, 8–12 mm long, with five 5–7 mm sepals; many flowers borne in branched groups of spike-like, 2–6 cm long clusters **Blooms:** July to September **Fruits:** 4 nutlets **Habitat:** disturbed sites **Distribution:** Eurasia; naturalized from Newfoundland to B.C., Alaska and Texas **Pick:** freely

Spotted Touch-Me-Not
Impatiens capensis

These delicate, dangling blooms have been likened to jewelled earrings; not surprisingly, the plant is also known as jewelweed. The flowers are designed to attract hummingbirds and hovering insects, but sometimes nectar thieves (usually bees) chew through the back of the flower to steal nectar. • The names *Impatiens* (meaning 'impatient') and touch-me-not both refer to the exploding pods of these plants. At the slightest touch, sometimes simply that of a passing breeze, the ripe pods suddenly recoil and shoot their seeds out in all directions. • This tender plant wilts quickly on hot summer days, but it isn't dying; it is just conserving water. • The mashed leaves were often applied externally to soothe rashes caused by neighbouring plants such as stinging nettle (p. 14) and poison-ivy (p. 15).

Plant: hairless annual 50–150 cm tall
Leaves: thin, soft, 3–10 cm long, toothed, long-stalked **Flowers:** golden orange with reddish brown spots, funnel-shaped with a flared mouth, 2–2.5 cm long, with 3 petals, 2 small, pale sepals and 1 large cone-shaped sepal tipped with a slender, curved tube (spur); flowers hanging in spreading clusters
Blooms: July to September **Fruits:** slender 2 cm pods, splitting lengthwise into 5 parts
Habitat: moist wooded or open sites
Distribution: native across Canada and throughout the eastern U.S. **Pick:** none

Early Blue Violet
Viola adunca

Early blue violet's delicate blossoms hold one of the loveliest wildflower fragrances. Enjoy it while you can. The flower's perfume doesn't fade, but your sense of smell is soon dulled by a substance called ionine. In a few moments the perfume returns, only to disappear again just as quickly. • The leaves and flowers of all violets are edible, but many wild species are too small for gathering. Violet flowers make beautiful garnishes in salads or punch bowls. They can also be candied or used to make purplish jelly and vinegar. • Violet leaves contain more vitamin A than spinach, and one-half cup of violet leaves has as much vitamin C as four oranges.

Plant: low perennial, 2–8 cm tall when flowering **Leaves:** basal (at flowering time), heart-shaped, usually 1–2.5 cm wide, blunt-toothed; stalks with 2 slender, toothed lobes (stipules) **Flowers:** blue to purple with a white throat, 2-lipped, with 5 separate petals and a 4–6 mm backward-pointing spur; side-petals hairy, 8–15 mm long; flowers single on slender stalks **Blooms:** May to July **Fruits:** 4–5 mm long capsules, shooting out brown seeds **Habitat:** moist to dry, sandy or gravelly sites **Distribution:** native from Labrador to Alaska, south through the western U.S. **Pick:** a few

Beach Pea
Lathyrus japonicus

This circumpolar plant is eaten around the world, and it has been credited with saving the lives of starving English country folk and arctic sailors. The sweet, tender young pods are edible both raw and cooked. The mature seeds, however, are best boiled in soup, ground into flour or roasted as a coffee substitute because they are hard to digest and may contain toxins. When people eat only *Lathyrus* plants for long periods (10–30 days), a condition called lathyrism may result. It can cause permanent paralysis along with several reversible disorders. Even common garden peas *(Pisum sativum)* can cause nervous disorders if eaten in large quantities for long periods. • The seeds of this very salt-tolerant plant can float for many kilometres on the ocean and start new plants when washed ashore again. • Beach pea has also been called *L. maritimus*.

Plant: clambering, blue-tinged perennial about 30–60 cm tall, with angled stems
Leaves: somewhat fleshy, tipped with a branched tendril above 6–12 large (3–5 cm), bristle-tipped leaflets and 2 large, symmetrical lobes (stipules) at base of stalk
Flowers: pinkish purple, pea-like, 1.5–2.5 cm long; in long-stalked clusters of 5–10
Blooms: June to August **Fruits:** veiny, pea-like pods about 5 cm long **Habitat:** beaches and gravelly shores **Distribution:** native in eastern temperate North America, along North American coasts and around the world **Pick:** a few

Perennial Sweet Pea
Lathyrus latifolius

Perennial sweet pea is native to southern Europe, but this hardy plant often escapes from gardens in North America to grow wild. With its showy flowers, perennial sweet pea is planted as an ornamental in Canada, but in Asia it is grown for food. The young shoots and pods are parboiled and eaten as cooked greens, and the seeds are boiled or roasted as a starchy vegetable. • The lower lip of each flower contains a specialized style that looks just like a tiny toothbrush. When an insect lands, this little brush sweeps pollen out from between the lower petals and onto the belly of its visitor. Press down on the upper side of a flower and watch the brush pop out.

Plant: clambering perennial up to 2 m tall, with broadly winged stems **Leaves:** tipped with a branched tendril above 2 large (4–8 cm) leaflets and 2 large (2.5–4 cm) lobes (stipules) at base of stalk; stalks winged **Flowers:** pink, purple or white, pea-like, 1.5–3 cm long; in elongating clusters of 4–10 flowers **Blooms:** June to August **Fruits:** 10- to 15-seeded, pea-like pods, 6–10 cm long **Habitat:** disturbed sites **Distribution:** Europe; naturalized across the U.S., southeastern Canada and B.C. **Pick:** freely

Bird Vetch
Vicia cracca

This abundant weed often goes unnoticed until it bursts into bloom in midsummer. Bees and butterflies flock to the nectar-rich flowers. When an insect lands, its weight forces the flower's inner parts to flip out from the lower lip. The female part then brushes pollen from the insect's belly, and the male part applies a fresh dusting of pollen. Pollinated flowers soon close, darken and point downwards. The mature pods burst when touched, each side recoiling tightly. You may not see the seeds shoot out, but you often hear them landing. • The young plants, pods and seeds are occasionally eaten, but they must be boiled first to destroy their toxins.

Plant: twining, grey-green perennial up to 1 m tall **Leaves:** pinnately divided, with 1–3 tendrils at the tip and 10–24 smooth-edged, sharp-pointed leaflets below, plus 2 lobes (stipules) at base of stalk **Flowers:** blue to lavender (rarely white), narrowly pea-like, 8–13 mm long, with unequal sepals and a bottlebrush-tipped style; flowers in dense, 1-sided clusters **Blooms:** June to August **Fruits:** slender, pea-like pods, 2–2.5 cm long, containing 5–8 seeds **Habitat:** disturbed ground **Distribution:** Eurasia; naturalized across North America **Pick:** freely

Bigleaf Lupine

Lupinus polyphyllus

This tall, showy wildflower is planted around the world as an ornamental. Cultivars with many different flower colours have been developed and are popular in temperate flower gardens. The hardy plants often escape from gardens, and wild populations are becoming abundant in parts of eastern North America. • The genus was named after the wolf, *lupus*, because its plants were believed to rob the soil of nourishment. In fact, lupine roots contain nitrogen-fixing bacteria that allow these plants to colonize and enrich extremely poor soil (see p. 44). • Bigleaf lupine is poisonous to people and livestock (especially sheep). Its beautiful flowers and pea-like seeds are the most dangerous parts.

Plant: clumped, hollow-stemmed perennial 50–150 cm tall
Leaves: palmately divided with 10–17 leaflets 4–13 cm long, on a 6–60 cm leaf stalk (upper stalks shorter)
Flowers: violet blue, pea-like, 1.2–1.6 cm long, with hairless petals; usually in rings (whorled) in dense, 20–40 cm long clusters **Blooms:** June to early September
Fruits: plump, curved, densely hairy pods, 3–5 cm long
Habitat: disturbed sites **Distribution:** native in western North America; naturalized in the northeastern U.S. and adjacent Canada **Pick:** freely

Purple Crown-Vetch
Coronilla varia

A native of the Mediterranean region, purple crown-vetch is now widely planted to cover bare ground and prevent erosion on exposed slopes. Its masses of pink flowers often blanket roadsides with a thick, pink carpet. The name *Coronilla*, 'small crown,' describes the beautiful flower clusters. • Like other members of the pea family, purple crown-vetch enriches the soil. Most poor soils lack nitrogen, and crown-vetch roots produce small nodules containing specialized bacteria that change nitrogen from the air into a form plants can use. Eventually, the crown-vetch dies and decomposes, and its captured nitrogen is added to the soil along with other nutrients accumulated by the plant.

Plant: sprawling to loosely ascending perennial 30–60 cm tall **Leaves:** pinnately divided into 11–25 smooth-edged, 1.2–2 cm long, oblong leaflets, stalkless **Flowers:** pink and white, pea-like, 1–1.5 cm long, with 5 sepals; 10–20 flowers in compact, head-like clusters about 2.5 cm wide **Blooms:** June to August **Fruits:** slender, 3- to 7-jointed, 4-sided pods, 2–6 cm long **Habitat:** disturbed ground **Distribution:** Europe; naturalized across temperate Canada (except Saskatchewan) and through the U.S. **Pick:** freely

Bird's-Foot Trefoil

Lotus corniculatus

This cheerful roadside wild-flower was brought to North America for fodder and honey. In the Middle Ages, bird's-foot trefoil was recommended as a potherb, but eventually it fell out of favour, perhaps because the raw leaves and flowers contain cyanide. Nineteenth-century herbalists began recommending the plant as a sedative when a distressed woman tried to use it to treat her inflamed eyes and instead found herself cured of insomnia and heart palpitations. No medicinal uses have been clinically proven. • *Corniculatus*, meaning 'small horn,' may refer to the tiny, pointed seed pods. Many fanciful common names for this weed compare its slender, spreading pods to toes or fingers. 'Trefoil' comes from the Latin *tria foliola*, which means 'three leaflets' —although this particular trefoil has five leaflets.

Plant: erect to sprawling perennial 10–60 cm tall **Leaves:** with 5 ovate, 5–15 mm long leaflets (3 at the tip and 2 near the stalk base) **Flowers:** bright yellow, sometimes tinged red, pea-like, 1–2 cm long; 3–6 flowers in flat-topped clusters on slender, 5–10 cm stalks **Blooms:** June to August **Fruits:** slender pods about 2.5 cm long, palmately arranged **Habitat:** moist, disturbed sites **Distribution:** Eurasia; naturalized across temperate Canada (except Saskatchewan) and through the U.S. **Pick:** freely

Sweet-Clover
Melilotus officinalis

Sweet-clover is a hardy, drought-resistant forage crop, known for its ability to improve poor soils. It is also highly valued as a honey plant, hence the name *Melilotus*, from the Greek *meli*, 'honey.' Its abundant, fragrant flowers produce large amounts of nectar. Once pollinated, a plant can produce as many as 350,000 seeds, some capable of surviving for more than 80 years. • Sweet-clover leaves and flowers emit a vanilla-like scent and have been used to enhance desserts and drinks, especially teas. The leaves also flavour Gruyère cheese, snuff and tobacco. However, only dry plants should be used for these purposes. Mouldy sweet-clover contains the toxic anti-clotting agent dicoumarin, which was used to develop the rodent poison warfarin. • White-flowered sweet-clover has been called *M. alba*.

Plant: slender, taprooted biennial (sometimes annual) with branched stems 50–200 cm tall **Leaves:** with 3 oblong to lance-shaped, blunt-tipped, 1–2.5 cm leaflets, sharply toothed on the upper half **Flowers:** yellow or white, narrowly pea-like, 4.5–7 mm long; in many narrow, 3–8 cm long clusters **Blooms:** May to September **Fruits:** egg-shaped pods about 3 mm long, usually 2-seeded **Habitat:** open, disturbed ground **Distribution:** Europe; naturalized across North America **Pick:** freely

Alfalfa
Medicago sativa

Alfalfa is a valuable fodder and green-manure plant that originally came from western Asia. It was planted in Greece as early as 490 BC; Spanish conquistadors later introduced it to Mexico and Chile. Nowadays, alfalfa is perhaps best known for its tender, delicately flavoured sprouts, which are popular in salads and sandwiches. The mature plants are rich in protein, trace minerals, vitamins (A, C, D, E and K), folic acid and fibre. They have been used to make a nutritious but rather tasteless tea for treating many ailments, from water retention to cancer. None of these various medicinal uses, though, has been clinically proven. Alfalfa should be consumed in moderation because it contains substances that may affect liver function and sensitivity of the skin to sun. • 'Alfalfa' is a Spanish word originally derived from the Arabic *al-fasfasah*, 'best fodder.'

Plant: deep-rooted perennial up to 1 m tall
Leaves: with three 1.5–3 cm leaflets (each tipped with teeth) and 2 slender, toothed lobes (stipules) at base of stalk
Flowers: violet blue (var. sativa) or yellow (var. falcata), 6–12 mm long, on 2–3 mm stalks, narrowly pea-like, with 5 petals and 5 slender sepals; flowers in dense, round to cylindrical, stalked clusters **Blooms:** June to September **Fruits:** small pods, tightly coiled in 1.5–4 complete turns **Habitat:** disturbed ground **Distribution:** Eurasia; naturalized across North America **Pick:** freely

Rabbitfoot Clover
Trifolium arvense

One glance at these furry flower clusters explains the 'rabbit-foot' in the name. This fuzzy plant usually grows where few others can: on very poor soil in dry locations. Densely hairy, relatively narrow leaflets help rabbitfoot clover conserve moisture. This little plant also boasts a well-developed root system that maximizes moisture uptake. Taproots will stretch down to 20 cm to reach buried water reserves, while spreading fibrous roots intercept available moisture near the ground surface. • Unlike most common clovers, rabbitfoot clover is an annual species, so it has to re-grow each year from seed. The bristly cup at the base of each tiny pod encourages seed dispersal by carrying the pod in the wind and by catching on passing animals.

Plant: soft-hairy, freely branched annual 10–40 cm tall **Leaves:** with 3 slender, 1–2 cm leaflets and 2 small, tapered, basal lobes (stipules); leaves stalkless upwards on the stem **Flowers:** fuzzy, about 6 mm long, with 5 inconspicuous, white or pinkish petals and 5 silky-hairy, bristle-like sepals; flowers in dense, stalked clusters 1–3 cm long **Blooms:** May to September **Fruits:** inconspicuous, straight, 1–6-seeded pods **Habitat:** sandy, disturbed ground **Distribution:** Eurasia and northern Africa; naturalized across the U.S. and southern Canada **Pick:** freely

Alsike Clover
Trifolium hybridum

Carpets of alsike clover stabilize the poor soils along many roads. This plant also improves the soil because clover roots have small nodules with specialized nitrogen-fixing bacteria (see p. 44). • Alsike clover is widely planted for fodder, food and medicine. The whole plant is rich in protein but difficult to digest, especially in large quantities; boiling helps. The tender white flower bases make a sweet nibble, and the dried flowerheads are used to make tea or are ground into flour. Research suggests that blood thinners found in clover may be useful for treating heart disease. • Each so-called 'flower' is actually a compact cluster of many tiny tubular flowers. These flowerheads bloom from the bottom up, and once pollinated, the flowers droop down, forming a skirt around the base of the cluster.

Plant: perennial 30–80 cm tall
Leaves: with 3 blunt-tipped, elliptic leaflets and 2 conspicuous, slender-tipped lobes (stipules) at base of stalk; upper leaves with shorter stalks **Flowers:** pinkish to white (brown with age), 7–10 mm long, distinctly stalked, narrowly pea-like, with 5 petals and 5 slender sepals; flowers in head-like clusters on 2–8 cm stalks **Blooms:** May to August
Fruits: inconspicuous, 1- to 6-seeded pods
Habitat: disturbed ground **Distribution:** Eurasia; naturalized across North America
Pick: freely

Red Clover
Trifolium pratense

I f you're looking for a lucky four-leaved clover, try searching a patch of red clover. Not only are four-parted leaves more common in this species, they are also extra large. This European native is often planted for forage and for green manure. Its long, tubular flowers depend on long-tongued bumble-bees for pollination, so when red clover was introduced to New Zealand and Australia, crops failed until bumblebees were imported too. This species is seldom used for food today, but whole plants, young leaves and flowers are all said to be edible, though difficult to digest. Never consume red clover in autumn, when it may look normal but contain toxic compounds. • Red clover has long been used medicinally, in cough remedies and as a tonic, sedative and anticancer agent.

Plant: short-lived perennial up to 80 cm tall
Leaves: with 3 ovate leaflets (broadest above the middle) and 2 slender-pointed basal stalk lobes (stipules); upper leaves short-stalked **Flowers:** magenta to almost white, 1.3–2 cm long, stalkless, narrowly pea-like, with 5 petals and 5 slender sepals; flowers in stalkless or short-stalked, 1.3–2.5 cm long heads **Blooms:** May to August
Fruits: inconspicuous, 1- to 6-seeded pods
Habitat: disturbed ground
Distribution: Europe; naturalized across North America **Pick:** freely

English Plantain
Plantago lanceolata

The raw leaves of this widely distributed weed have a mild, mushroom-like flavour. The young, tender leaves are sometimes used in salads, and older leaves are cooked as a vegetable or potherb. When the seeds are soaked in water, they produce a clear, sticky substance (mucilage) that helps them to catch on passing animals and travel to new sites. This gum has been used in lotions and hair-wave products. Mucilage is soothing, so plantain seeds were traditionally used as a laxative and in teas for coughs and diarrhea. The leaves soothe cuts, blisters, burns and bites. The Saxons even bound English plantain to their heads to treat headaches. • Plantain flowers develop in a tight spiral, starting at the spike base. The inconspicuous female parts develop first, followed by a showy ring of stamens. • This plant is also known as ribwort because of its ribbed stems and leaves.

Plant: erect perennial with grooved, 15–60 cm stalks from tan-woolly bases with fibrous roots **Leaves:** basal, 10–40 cm long and less than $\frac{1}{6}$ as wide, with 3 to several ribs **Flowers:** tiny, greenish white, with 4 long stamens; flowers in axils of thin bracts, in 1.5–8 cm spikes **Blooms:** May to October **Fruits:** 2-seeded capsules, 3–4 mm long, with tops splitting off **Habitat:** moist, disturbed sites **Distribution:** Eurasia; naturalized from Newfoundland to B.C., Alaska and Texas **Pick:** freely

Common Teasel
Dipsacus fullonum

In England, common teasel was planted for use in the French, German, Italian and African wool industries. Teasel cultivation also became a sizable industry in New York state. One hectare could yield about 14 cubic metres of teasel heads. The dried flowerheads were fastened to the rim of a cylinder, which was revolved over the wool fabric to tease the cloth and raise the nap. Teasel spines had the ideal combination of stiffness and elasticity needed to raise the nap without tearing the fabric. Later, hooked bristles like those found on teasel inspired the invention of Velcro. • Wild teasel *(D. fullonum* ssp. *sylvestris)* has straight bristles, and the planted teasel *(D. fullonum* ssp. *fullonum)* has hooked bristles. The domesticated form may revert to growing straighter bristles if it escapes cultivation and grows wild.

Plant: prickly biennial 50–200 cm tall, from taproot **Leaves:** paired, lance-shaped, 10–30 cm long, often joined in a cup around the stem **Flowers:** lavender, pinkish or white, trumpet-shaped, 1–1.5 cm long, soon fading and hidden by spine-tipped bracts in dense, egg-shaped, 3–10 cm flowerheads above a circle (whorl) of slender, upcurved bracts **Blooms:** July to September **Fruits:** 8-ribbed, seed-like achenes, 5 mm long **Habitat:** moist, disturbed sites **Distribution:** Europe; naturalized in Ontario, Quebec, B.C. and across the U.S. **Pick:** freely

Lesser Burdock
Arctium minus

Lesser burdock arrived in New England in 1638, and by 1860 its sticky seed heads had carried it to most Ontario farms and towns. As a medicine, this burdock and others were used to treat everything from kidney problems and rheumatism to psoriasis and dizziness. The large leaves provided poultices for skin problems, and the seeds were applied to bruises, venomous bites, abscesses and smallpox sores. • The fleshy taproots of first-year plants can be eaten raw or boiled as a vegetable. Burdock roots have also been dried, roasted until brown and ground as a coffee substitute. Like artichokes, burdock roots contain the complex carbohydrate inulin, which breaks down to fructose. The white stem pith is also edible raw, steamed, roasted, boiled or even simmered in sugar to make candy. *Note:* Pregnant women and diabetics should not use burdock.

Plant: coarse biennial with hollow stems 30–150 cm tall **Leaves:** somewhat woolly underneath, up to 50 cm long, ovate to heart-shaped, stalked **Flowerheads** bur-like, 1.5–2 cm across, with slender, pink or purplish tubular florets projecting from the tip of a spherical cluster of greenish to purplish, hooked bracts; flowerheads in branched, elongated clusters **Blooms:** July to October **Fruits:** seed-like achenes **Habitat:** disturbed sites **Distribution:** Eurasia; naturalized across the U.S. and southern Canada **Pick:** freely

Canada Thistle
Cirsium arvense

Despite its name, Canada thistle is not a native plant. It arrived here from Eurasia in the 1700s and spread south to the U.S., where it was given its common name. • This is our only thistle with colonies of male or female plants. Deep underground runners shoot out rapidly—up to 6 m per plant per year—sending up as many as 200 shoots in the first summer. New shoots often stand in lines radiating from the parent plant, but soon they grow their own runners, and the ground becomes blanketed in a thistle maze. One female plant can produce up to 40,000 seeds, each one capable of surviving 20 years or more. Not only can thistles reproduce rapidly, they have spiny leaves that are usually left to flourish, unmolested by grazing animals.

Plant: prickly perennial 30–150 cm tall
Leaves: sometimes white-woolly underneath, wavy-edged or lobed, spiny-toothed **Flowerheads:** rose purple to white, 1.5–2.5 cm across; florets all tubular, above a 1–2 cm cup of overlapping, pointed to spine-tipped bracts; flowerheads in branched clusters
Blooms: June to September **Fruits:** seed-like achenes with white, feathery bristles
Habitat: disturbed sites **Distribution:** Eurasia; naturalized from Newfoundland to Alaska to New Mexico **Pick:** freely; caution

Bull Thistle
Cirsium vulgare

Like other thistles, this showy immigrant is edible, but it does take skill to deal with the sharp prickles. Bull thistle is our spiniest species, and it should always be handled with gloves. The young leaves and stems are said to make excellent salad greens or cooked vegetables, but first they must be peeled of their spiny outer layers. Usually the roots of first-year plants are eaten, either raw or cooked. The best thistles taste like artichokes, but even tough, bitter, older plants can be eaten in an emergency. Most animals avoid these prickly plants, so thistles can become troublesome weeds but also abundant survival food. Thistles are very important to goldfinches, which eat the seeds while gathering fluff to line their nests. • *Cirsium* comes from the Greek for 'swollen vein,' a problem one thistle was used to treat.

Plant: biennial with spiny-winged stems 50–150 cm tall, sometimes cobwebby-hairy
Leaves: stiff-hairy on the upper side, spiny-toothed, with lower edges extending down the stem **Flowerheads:** rose purple, 4–5 cm across; florets all strap-like, above a 2.5–4 cm cluster of spine-tipped bracts; flowerheads single at branch tips
Blooms: June to September
Fruits: seed-like achenes, tipped with white, feathery bristles **Habitat:** disturbed sites
Distribution: Eurasia; naturalized from Newfoundland to Alaska to Texas
Pick: freely; caution

Nodding Plumeless-Thistle

Carduus nutans

This aggressive colonizer arrived in North America early in the 1900s and is now a troublesome weed. Nodding plumeless-thistle spreads rapidly by seed, sometimes forming extensive colonies that reduce crop and rangeland productivity by 100%. • In Europe, dried nodding-thistle flowers are still used to curdle milk in cheese-making, giving rise to another name, milk thistle. When mashed flowers are soaked in water for 5–6 hours and the liquid is added to warm (50° C) milk, the milk curdles in about 30 minutes. • Like true thistles (*Cirsium* spp.), plumeless-thistles taste rather like artichokes. With their spines removed, young stems, leaves and flower-heads can be eaten raw in salads or steamed and served hot.

Plant: erect biennial, with spiny-winged stems 30–200 cm tall **Leaves:** prickly, 7–25 cm long, irregularly sharp-toothed and lobed, with lower edges extending down the stem **Flowerheads:** rose purple, 4–6 cm across; florets all tubular, above overlapping rows of broad (2–8 mm), spine-tipped, down-curved bracts; flowerheads nodding, long-stalked, usually single **Blooms:** June to October **Fruits:** seed-like achenes with white, finely barbed bristles **Habitat:** disturbed sites **Distribution:** Eurasia; naturalized from Newfoundland to B.C. to Texas **Pick:** freely; caution

Spotted Knapweed
Centaurea biebersteinii

Spotted knapweed is a permanent member of many top 10 lists for noxious weeds. In Canada, it was first reported from Victoria, B.C., in 1893, and by 1932 it was found in Quebec. Although spotted knapweed is easily controlled by plowing, it has infested hundreds of thousands of acres of rangeland in western North America, and abundant stands have also been found in Ontario. These plants spread only by seed, but one plant can produce more than 20,000 seeds, each a potential new colony. Plants begin growing early in spring, and this head start helps them outstrip other species in the race for moisture, nutrients and light. Once established, they give off chemicals to prevent other plants from growing nearby.
• *C. biebersteinii* has also been called *C. maculosa*.

Plant: much-branched biennial or perennial 30–100 cm tall, sometimes with thin, cobwebby hairs
Leaves: pinnately cut into slender lobes
Flowerheads: pink-purple, 2–2.5 cm across; florets all tubular, but outer florets enlarged and spreading; flowerheads many, each with a 1–1.3 cm cluster of ribbed, black-fringed bracts **Blooms:** June to September **Fruits:** seed-like achenes
Habitat: disturbed sites **Distribution:** Europe; naturalized in eastern and western Canada and across the U.S. **Pick:** freely

Brown Knapweed
Centaurea jacea

This colourful European immigrant is almost as showy as its beautiful garden cousin, cornflower or bachelor's button *(C. cyanus)*. Brown knapweed was introduced to Quebec in the mid-1800s as a forage and hay plant that had the added benefit of providing abundant nectar for honey-bees. Although it was rare in its native Britain in the early 1900s, it has done well on this continent, spreading across much of eastern North America and now considered a pest in some areas. • Brown knapweed is no longer used medicinally, but in the 1600s herbalist Culpepper recommended it for treating bruises, asthma, coughs and diseases of the head and nerves.

Plant: erect perennial 20–70 cm tall, sometimes with thin, cobwebby hairs **Leaves:** slender, smooth-edged or toothed, reduced upwards **Flowerheads:** pink-purple, 2.5–4 cm across; florets all tubular, but outer florets enlarged and spreading; flowerheads many, each with a 1.2–1.8 cm high cluster of overlapping bracts with tan to dark brown, irregularly fringed or torn tips **Blooms:** June to September **Fruits:** seed-like achenes **Habitat:** disturbed sites **Distribution:** Europe; naturalized in eastern and western North America **Pick:** freely

Chicory
Cichorium intybus

This common weed has been planted in North America, India and Europe as food, fodder and a commercial source of sugar (fructose) and sugar-enhancer (maltol). The delicate blue florets add a colourful touch to salads. The tender young roots and leaves can be eaten raw in salads or cooked as a vegetable; the plants do, however, soon grow tough and bitter. The roots are considered one of the best caffeine-free substitutes or additives for coffee. Chopped chicory roots are dried, roasted until dark brown and ground. Sugars in the roots produce a distinctive, coffee-like fragrance when the roots are roasted. The grounds are used like coffee grounds, either alone or mixed with two parts coffee, and they are used as a tangy seasoning in stews and soups. Chicory roots should be harvested before or well after the plants have bloomed.

Plant: slender perennial 30–120 cm tall with stiff, widely branched stems, from deep taproot **Leaves:** mainly basal, dandelion-like, 8–20 cm long; smaller, simpler and fewer upwards **Flowerheads:** blue (sometimes pink or white), 2–4 cm across; florets all strap-like, with square tips; flowerheads essentially stalkless, 1–3 in upper leaf axils **Blooms:** June to October **Fruits:** 2–3 mm long, seed-like achenes tipped with tiny whitish scales **Habitat:** disturbed ground **Distribution:** Europe; naturalized from Newfoundland to B.C. to Texas **Pick:** freely

Tall Blue Lettuce
Lactuca biennis

The scientific name *Lactuca*, from the Latin *lac*, 'milk,' refers to the milky sap of plants in this genus. The sap was said to heal pimples and other skin problems, and the leaves were applied to soothe stings. People with sensitive skin, however, may develop rashes from contact with lettuce sap. Traditionally, tall blue lettuce leaves were used in teas taken as sedatives and nerve tonics; even Peter Rabbit knew how soporific lettuce can be. All lettuces produce juice with narcotic components, but its strength varies considerably, and tall blue lettuce is not one of the more potent species. Lettuce sap was once dried and rolled into small balls to produce a very opium-like substance, called lactarium, that was sometimes passed off as the real thing. Some Native people also used the roots in medicinal teas for stopping bleeding and treating diarrhea, nausea, pain and various heart and lung problems.

Plant: leafy annual or biennial 60–200 cm tall, from deep, spreading roots **Leaves:** 10–40 cm long, toothed and deeply lobed
Flowerheads: bluish to white, about 5 mm across, with 15–35 strap-like florets from a tubular, 1–1.5 cm long cluster of green bracts; flowerheads in narrow, branched clusters
Blooms: July to October **Fruits:** beakless, several-nerved, seed-like achenes, tipped with silky, pale brown parachutes **Habitat:** moist, usually disturbed sites **Distribution:** native across temperate North America; rare in Alaska, Alberta, Manitoba **Pick:** a few; caution

Prickly Lettuce
Lactuca serriola

Common garden lettuce *(L. sativa)* was probably developed from prickly lettuce. Young leaves of this plant have been eaten in salads or cooked as a vegetable, but they are usually too bitter for most tastes. The bitter, milky sap (latex) contains rubbery compounds, and prickly lettuce was once considered as a commercial source of rubber, but it proved uneconomical. Herbalists use the dried sap as a mild sedative and painkiller; it has even been used to cure opium addiction. Many sources recognize the weak narcotic qualities of lettuce sap, but studies supporting its use as a medicine are lacking. In any case, the tedious process of collecting and drying a usable amount of sap would require a great deal of patience. • Prickly lettuce is known as a 'compass plant'; the vertical upper leaves are said to align north–south.

Plant: bristly-prickly annual or biennial 30–150 cm tall **Leaves:** spiny-toothed, deeply lobed, often twisted to stand vertically on edge, upper leaves smaller and often clasping **Flowerheads:** yellow (drying blue), about 6 mm across, with 14–24 strap-like florets from a tubular, 1–1.5 cm long cluster of green bracts; flowerheads in many-branched clusters **Blooms:** July to September **Fruits:** spiny-ribbed, seed-like achenes with silky white parachutes on stalk-like beaks **Habitat:** disturbed sites **Distribution:** Eurasia; naturalized from Quebec to B.C. to Texas **Pick:** freely; caution

Hairy Cat's-Ear
Hypochaeris radicata

Historically, this small plant was grown as a vegetable in Europe and Asia. Some sources suggest that the mild-flavoured leaves can be eaten raw in salads, but given the hairiness of the plants, cat's-ear salad may be an acquired taste. The small flowerheads have been tossed into salads and used to make tea, wine and jelly. • Since its introduction to North America, hairy cat's-ear has spread rapidly across the continent. It could be mistaken for a small dandelion, but dandelions have thick, hollow stalks without bracts, and the fluffy parachutes on dandelion seeds have simple (not feathery) hairs. Like dandelion, hairy cat's-ear invades lawns and gardens, smothering nearby plants with spreading leaf rosettes.

Plant: erect, bristly-hairy perennial with milky sap, several-stemmed, 15–60 cm tall, from fibrous, sometimes thickened roots **Leaves:** basal, toothed to shallowly lobed, 3–35 cm long **Flowerheads:** yellow, 2.5 cm across; florets all strap-like, above a cluster of overlapping bracts; flowerheads in branched clusters **Blooms:** May to September **Fruits:** many-nerved, seed-like achenes tipped with slender beaks bearing parachutes of feathery hairs **Habitat:** disturbed sites **Distribution:** Eurasia; naturalized across temperate North America, except on the prairies **Pick:** freely

Yellow Hawkweed

Hieracium caespitosum

Yellow hawkweed is also known as king devil because it is a king among wayside weeds. Like its weedy cousin orange hawkweed (p. 64), yellow hawkweed reproduces by seeds, underground stems and runners. Hawkweeds have showy flowerheads that attract pollinating insects, but they can also produce abundant seed without fertilization, yielding offspring that are clones of the parent plant. This type of reproduction (apomixis) creates classification nightmares for scientists by producing thousands of almost identical plants. More than 400 minor species of *Hieracium* have been described from Britain and about 2000 from Scandinavia. • *H. caespitosum* has also been called *H. pratense* or meadow hawkweed.

Plant: erect, bristly-hairy perennial with milky sap, 1- to several-stemmed, 25–90 cm tall
Leaves: basal, tufted, 5–25 cm long
Flowerheads: bright yellow, 1–2 cm across; florets all strap-like, above a cluster of bracts with stiff, black, gland-tipped hairs; flowerheads in compact, branched clusters of 5–30
Blooms: May to August **Fruits:** ribbed, seed-like achenes tipped with a tuft of soft, brownish hairs **Habitat:** disturbed sites **Distribution:** Europe; naturalized in eastern North America and the northwestern U.S. **Pick:** freely

Orange Hawkweed

Hieracium aurantiacum

In Britain in the 1600s, orange hawkweed was planted as a novelty ornamental for its bright orange flowerheads and black, hairy stalks. Although it is not used as a medicine today, at that time orange hawkweed was boiled in water or wine, which was then drunk or applied externally to heal wounds. Today, this common wildflower is often called devil's paintbrush. Its flowerheads resemble tiny brushes dipped into orange paint, and it can be a devil of a weed. A very successful colonizer, orange hawkweed reproduces from seed, from spreading underground stems and from trailing runners.
• The name *Hieracium*, from the Greek *hieros*, 'hawk,' refers to the ancient myth that hawks ate these plants to improve their vision.

Plant: erect, bristly-hairy, 1- to several-stemmed perennial 10–60 cm tall, with milky sap **Leaves:** basal, tufted, 5–15 cm long **Flowerheads:** red-orange, 1.5–2.5 cm across; florets all strap-like, above a cluster of bracts with stiff, black, often gland-tipped hairs; flowerheads in compact, branched clusters of 5–30 **Blooms:** June to August **Fruits:** ribbed, seed-like achenes with a tuft of soft, brownish hairs **Habitat:** disturbed sites **Distribution:** Europe; naturalized in southeastern Canada and the northeastern U.S. **Pick:** freely

Perennial Sow-Thistle

Sonchus arvensis

Some say the young shoots and leaves of this common weed provide one of the best wild salads, but older leaves and flower buds are best boiled for 5–10 minutes. The bright yellow flowerheads provide a colourful garnish. • Perennial sow-thistle spreads rapidly. A single plant can produce 4000 seeds, which mature in only 10 days and can survive for several years. Once they establish, the fleshy, white roots spread horizontally, sending up new shoots. The roots are easily broken, and even small pieces can produce new plants. Additional roots stretch down as deep as 3 m. Sow-thistle competes enthusiastically for nutrients, moisture and light, so even minor infestations can drastically reduce crop yields. • Sow-thistle was so named because pigs apparently like to eat it.

Plant: erect, often blue-green perennial 40–200 cm tall, with milky sap **Leaves:** 6–40 cm long, with prickly, deeply lobed edges; smaller, less lobed and clasping upwards on the stem **Flowerheads:** yellow, 3–5 cm across; florets all strap-like, above overlapping rows of slender green bracts; flowerheads in widely branched clusters **Blooms:** July to October **Fruits:** wrinkled, 10-ribbed, seed-like achenes tipped with silky white parachutes **Habitat:** disturbed sites **Distribution:** Europe; naturalized from Newfoundland to Alaska to Texas **Pick:** freely

Common Dandelion
Taraxacum officinale

This successful immigrant has been planted for food and medicine since ancient times in Europe, China and India. The tender young leaves, rich in vitamins and minerals, make good salad or cooked greens. The delicate yellow flowers can be added to fritters and pancakes or made into wine. Dandelion roots provide a raw or cooked vegetable, a caffeine-free coffee substitute or even a red dye. With age, the plants soon grow bitter; leaves in full sun are especially harsh. Pale plants (like those grown in shade or buried in sand) and frost-nipped plants are sweetest. The mildly laxative and diuretic leaves have been used in medicinal teas, digestive aids, diet drinks and rustic beers.

Plant: robust perennial with milky juice, 5–50 cm tall, from taproot **Leaves:** basal, 5–40 cm long, irregularly toothed and lobed **Flowerheads:** yellow, 2–5 cm across; florets strap-like, above 2 rows of slender, green bracts, the outer row bent backwards; flowerheads single on leafless, hollow stalks **Blooms:** April to September **Fruits:** spiny-ribbed, seed-like achenes with a slender, stalk-like beak bearing a silky, white parachute **Habitat:** disturbed sites **Distribution:** Eurasia; a cosmopolitan weed **Pick:** freely

Common Goat's-Beard
Tragopogon dubius

Look for common goat's-beard early and late in the day. Its flowerheads usually open at sunrise and close by midday, but the large, fluffy seed heads are most visible in the evening, when their silky hairs catch the rays of the setting sun. The names goat's-beard and *Tragopogon* (from the Greek *tragos*, 'billy goat' and *pôgôn*, 'beard') both refer to the fluffy tufts of hair on the seeds. These downy parachutes often carry seeds over great distances on the wind, rapidly spreading the plant to new areas. • Tender young goat's-beard shoots are edible raw or cooked, the same way as asparagus, and the plant bases are sometimes cooked like artichokes. Also, the fleshy roots of first-year plants have been roasted or boiled like parsnips.

Plant: erect biennial 30–100 cm tall, with milky sap **Leaves:** grass-like, tapered from a clasping base to a slender point **Flowerheads:** yellow, 2.5–6.5 cm across; florets all strap-like, above longer, slender-pointed, green bracts; flowerheads borne on swollen stalk tips **Blooms:** May to August **Fruits:** ribbed, seed-like achenes, 2.5–3.5 cm long, with a stout beak supporting a parachute of feathery white hairs **Habitat:** open, disturbed sites **Distribution:** Europe; naturalized from Newfoundland to Alaska to Texas **Pick:** freely

Annual Sunflower

Helianthus annuus

Annual sunflower was one of the first plants cultivated in North America. Its oily seeds were usually roasted, shelled and ground into meal for making gruel or bread. Often this meal was mixed with fat and formed into flat cakes. Today, sunflower seeds are popular in breads, cereals, salads and many other dishes. Although we usually think of only the seeds as edible, the bright yellow strap-like florets make a colourful salad garnish. The leaves and immature flowerheads provide a vegetable with an artichoke-like flavour. In the 1600s, they were said to equal artichokes in flavour and to surpass them in procuring bodily lust. • The name *Helianthus*, 'sun flower,' refers to the fact that the flowerheads constantly turn to face the sun.

Plant: coarse, rough-hairy annual plant 50–300 cm tall **Leaves:** mostly alternate, ovate to heart-shaped, 6–25 cm long, usually toothed and stalked **Flowerheads:** yellow, 5–15 cm across; many strap-like florets surrounding a 3–4 cm, red-brown button of tubular florets, with broad, abruptly slender-pointed bracts at the base; 1 to few flowerheads **Blooms:** July to September **Fruits:** 2–4-sided, seed-like achenes, 5–10 mm long, containing a white seed **Habitat:** moist, disturbed sites **Distribution:** native in the western U.S.; naturalized across North America and around the world **Pick:** freely

Elecampane
Inula helenium

Elecampane was brought to North America for food and human medicine and to treat livestock skin diseases. Although elecampane is edible, it is very aromatic and strong-flavoured. The roots have usually been cut up like ginger and used to flavour spice cake, fruit salad and other desserts. They have also been boiled in syrup to make a candy said to stimulate digestion and ease coughs. The bright yellow strap-like florets make a flavourful garnish in salads and desserts. Like many aromatic herbs, elecampane has been used as a medicine since ancient times, but the risk of allergic reactions is too high to justify its use. Pregnant women should definitely avoid it.
• This tall, sunflower-like plant makes a striking garden flower.

Plant: hairy perennial 60–200 cm tall, from thick roots **Leaves:** woolly underneath, shallowly toothed, 25–50 cm long, stalked; upper leaves smaller, stalkless, often clasping **Flowerheads:** yellow, 5–10 cm across; many strap-like florets surrounding a button of tubular florets, with large, leafy bracts at the base; 1 to few flowerheads **Blooms:** June to August **Fruits:** 4-sided, seed-like achenes tipped with soft, tufted hairs
Habitat: moist to wet disturbed sites
Distribution: Eurasia; naturalized in eastern and western North America
Pick: freely

Black-Eyed Susan
Rudbeckia hirta

Black-eyed Susan is native to the American Midwest, but in the past 100 years it has spread rapidly, probably with hay and livestock, and it is now common from coast to coast. The cheerful orange and brown flowerheads make excellent, long-lasting cut flowers. Be sure, though, to take a pair of scissors along if you want to gather a bouquet because the stems are quite tough. The blossoms also make lovely pressed flowers and winter bouquets because they keep their bright orange colour when dried. Black-eyed Susan cultivars may be found at most gardening centres. • The brown tubular florets produce bright yellow pollen. Outer florets mature first, and a thin yellow ring of pollen gradually moves toward the centre of the disc. • This species has also been called *R. serotina*.

Plant: rough-hairy biennial or short-lived perennial 30–100 cm tall **Leaves:** 5–17 cm long, ovate to narrowly oblong, with winged stalks; upper leaves stalkless
Flowerheads: orange-yellow, 5–10 cm across, with 10–20 orange to golden yellow strap-like florets around a dark purple to brown, 1.2–2 cm wide hemisphere or cone of tubular florets; 1 to few flowerheads **Blooms:** June to September
Fruits: seed-like achenes **Habitat:** open, often disturbed sites **Distribution:** central North America; naturalized from Newfoundland to B.C. to Mexico **Pick:** freely

Oxeye Daisy
Leucanthemum vulgare

This highly successful weed originated in Asia and spread into Europe hundreds of years ago. First introduced to eastern North America in the early 1600s, it is now one of the most common wildflowers across the continent. Many travellers enjoy the cheerful blooms, which fill ditches and blanket fields, but farmers view oxeye daisy as an aggressive weed that rapidly replaces valuable forage plants. • Daisies have long been part of European lore, twisted into daisy chains and circlets at picnics and school commencements, or plucked of their white 'petals' (actually strap-like florets) to the chant 'He loves me, he loves me not.' • This species previously had a lovely rhyming name, *Chrysanthemum leucanthemum*.

Plant: slender, erect perennial 20–90 cm tall, from spreading rootstock **Leaves:** basal and alternate, 4–15 cm long, coarsely toothed or lobed, smaller and stalkless upwards **Flowerheads:** white, 2.5–5 cm across; 15–35 strap-like florets around a bright yellow, 1–2 cm button of tubular florets, with dry, brown-edged bracts at the base; flowerheads single **Blooms:** May to September **Fruits:** 10-ribbed, seed-like achenes **Habitat:** open, disturbed sites **Distribution:** Eurasia; naturalized from Newfoundland to Alaska to Texas **Pick:** freely

Scentless Chamomile
Tripleurospermum perforata

An aggressive invader of pastures and of hay fields, scentless chamomile sometimes infests cropland. Today, this flourishing immigrant is classified as a noxious weed across western Canada and Quebec. A single plant can produce more than 300,000 seeds, which may remain dormant for several years, waiting until the time is right to germinate and produce a whole new generation of plants. • At first glance, this species could easily be mistaken for oxeye daisy (p. 71), but upon a closer examination, the finely divided leaves will clearly identify scentless chamomile. A similar weedy species, stinking chamomile *(Anthemis cotula)*, is easily distinguished by its foul smell. • *T. perforata* has also been called *Matricaria perforata* and *M. maritima* (in part).

Plant: erect, nearly scentless annual (usually), biennial or short-lived perennial 10–70 cm tall **Leaves:** 2–8 cm long, pinnately divided into slender, often thread-like parts **Flowerheads:** white, 2.5–5 cm across; 12–25 strap-like florets around a bright yellow, 8–15 mm hemisphere of tubular florets; several to many flowerheads **Blooms:** July to September **Fruits:** rectangular, 3-ribbed, seed-like achenes **Habitat:** open, disturbed sites **Distribution:** Eurasia; naturalized from Newfoundland to Alaska to the central U.S. **Pick:** freely

Pineapple-Weed
Matricaria discoidea

T his aromatic herb is closely related to chamomile *(M. recutita)* and has been used in many of the same ways. Bruised pineapple-weed smells like freshly cut pineapple. The fragrant plants make an excellent deodorant, capable of masking even the strong smell of fish when rubbed on hands. Pineapple-weed can also be hung as an air freshener, stuffed into pillows and sachets, dropped into hot bath water for an aromatic soak or rubbed over skin or clothing as perfume and insect repellent. The flowerheads can be nibbled straight from the plant, tossed into salads as a lemony garnish or steeped in water to make a fragrant tea. The tea acts as a mild sedative for inducing sleep and soothing upset stomachs. • *M. discoidea* has also been called *M. matricarioides*.

Plant: leafy, low-branching annual 5–40 cm tall
Leaves: 1–5 cm long, 2–3 times pinnately divided into slender, sometimes thread-like parts **Flowerheads:** yellow, 5–9 mm across, cone-shaped; florets all tubular, above dry, thin-edged bracts; several to many flowerheads **Blooms:** May to September **Fruits:** 2-ribbed, often 5-sided, seed-like achenes **Habitat:** open, disturbed sites **Distribution:** native in the western cordillera; naturalized across most of North America **Pick:** freely

Common Tansy
Tanacetum vulgare

Common tansy was one of the first medicinal herbs brought to North America. Traditionally it was used to repel lice and fleas, kill intestinal worms and induce abortions, sometimes with fatal results for both mother and child. It has also been used to flavour liqueurs, cakes, puddings, omelets, salads and cheeses, but now we know it should never be used in food unless its toxins (especially thujone) have been removed. • Common tansy was the herb that made Ganymede, beautiful cup-bearer of the Greek gods, immortal. For that reason, and because of its strong, insect-repelling fragrance, this plant was used to preserve bodies in ancient Greece. • In Canada, common tansy is a troublesome weed. One plant can produce more than 50,000 seeds, and established plants spread rapidly with creeping rootstocks.

Plant: coarse, leafy, aromatic perennial 40–100 cm tall **Leaves:** dotted with glands, 10–20 cm long, pinnately divided into deeply lobed and/or sharply toothed leaflets; short-stalked to stalkless **Flowerheads:** deep yellow, 5–10 mm across; florets all tubular; flowerheads in flat-topped clusters of 20–200 **Blooms:** July to September **Fruits:** 5-ribbed, seed-like achenes **Habitat:** disturbed sites **Distribution:** Eurasia; naturalized across most of North America **Pick:** freely

Canada Goldenrod
Solidago canadensis

This eye-catching wildflower has been much maligned as the guilty party in countless hay fever attacks. In fact, goldenrod pollen is too heavy to travel on the wind; insects must carry it from flower to flower. The real hay fever culprits are inconspicuous plants, such as ragweeds (*Ambrosia* species), that grow nearby and flower at the same time. Plants with wind-pollinated flowers often go unnoticed because they don't have showy flowers. • Some large goldenrod colonies are estimated to be about 100 years old. Older, central plants may eventually die back, creating a ring, but usually colonies are too dense for other plants to invade. • Beautiful Canada goldenrod is rarely grown in Canadian gardens, but it is apparently popular in Europe.

Plant: perennial 25–200 cm tall with finely hairy upper stems, from spreading rootstock
Leaves: 3–15 cm long, 5–20 mm wide, toothed, finely hairy underneath (at least on main veins), stalkless **Flowerheads:** yellow, 2–4 mm across; 10–17 strap-like florets and 2–8 tubular florets above overlapping, green-tipped bracts; flowerheads on 1-sided branches in pyramidal clusters
Blooms: August to October **Fruits:** seed-like achenes tipped with tufted white hairs
Habitat: open sites **Distribution:** native from Newfoundland to Alaska to Texas **Pick:** a few

Common Yarrow
Achillea millefolium

In the Middle Ages, common yarrow was found in every monastery, apothecary shop and household medicine chest, ready to treat anyone who admitted to illness. It was used most often to stimulate sweating, reduce inflammation and stop bleeding. The fresh, young leaves also supplied a rather bitter, aromatic salad green. When eaten today, the young leaves are often cooked as a vegetable or potherb, and the older leaves provide a sage-like seasoning or a nourishing tea. Housewives and wild birds alike have used this pungent plant to repel insects, such as fleas. Smoke from burning yarrow flowers was said to repel both insects and evil spirits, and smouldering seed heads were used to keep witches at bay.

Plant: aromatic perennial 20–100 cm tall, from spreading rootstock **Leaves:** feathery, 3–15 cm long, finely divided, often grey-hairy **Flowerheads:** white to pink, 5–6 mm across; 4–6 short strap-like florets around 10–30 yellow tubular florets above overlapping, dark-edged bracts; flowerheads in flat-topped, 2–10 cm wide clusters **Blooms:** June to September **Fruits:** hairless, flattened, seed-like achenes **Habitat:** highly variable; often disturbed sites **Distribution:** native throughout North America and around the world **Pick:** a few

Pearly Everlasting
Anaphalis margaritacea

This native species was long ago exported to Europe, and by the late 1600s it was common in English gardens. In Canada, dried plants were added to smoking mixtures, both as a medicine and as a tobacco substitute. Some tribes used pearly everlasting tea to treat coughs, colds and digestive upsets. They also smoked the leaves to relieve throat and lung problems. The fuzzy leaves were used in poultices for burns, sores, bruises, swellings and rheumatism. In the west, warriors rubbed the chewed plants onto their bodies for strength, energy and protection from danger. • The name *margaritacea*, derived from the Greek *margarites*, 'pearl,' refers to the pearly flowerheads, which look beautiful in dried-flower arrangements. Once dried, the blooms are indeed everlasting.

Plant: loosely white-woolly, leafy perennial 30–90 cm tall, from spreading rootstock **Leaves:** 2–12 cm long, stalkless, densely woolly underneath **Flowerheads:** pearly white, 5–10 mm across, with papery, petal-like bracts around a cluster of yellow or brownish tubular florets; flowerheads in dense, flat-topped clusters **Blooms:** July to August **Fruits:** rough, seed-like achenes tipped with short, white hairs **Habitat:** dry, open, often disturbed sites **Distribution:** native from Newfoundland to Alaska to New Mexico and in eastern Asia; rare in Saskatchewan and the North **Pick:** a few

Fringed Aster
Aster ciliolatus

This cheerful blue wildflower brightens waysides long after most other blooms have faded. Many different asters grow wild in Ontario, but fringed aster is one of the easiest to identify. It has distinctive heart-shaped lower leaves with long, fringed stalks.
• Native peoples sometimes used fringed aster for medicine. They boiled the strongly scented roots to make eye drops, and they used the smoke from burning roots to revive people who had fainted in sweat baths. Sometimes a paper cone was used to force the smoke from smouldering asters up the nose of an unconscious patient.
• *A. ciliolatus* may also be called *Symphyotrichum ciliolatum*. The genus name *Aster* means 'star,' aptly describing the many-rayed flowerheads.

Plant: erect perennial 20–120 cm tall, from spreading rootstock **Leaves:** 4–12 cm long, pointed; lowest leaves toothed, heart-shaped, with notched bases and slender, hairy-edged stalks; stem leaves lance-shaped, usually stalkless **Flowerheads:** pale blue to purplish, 1.5–3 cm across; 12–25 strap-like florets around a button of yellow tubular florets, with slender bracts at the base; flowerheads in branched, open clusters **Blooms:** July to October **Fruits:** seed-like achenes tipped with a parachute of silky white hairs **Habitat:** woodlands and open, often disturbed sites **Distribution:** Quebec to B.C., south to the northern U.S. **Pick:** a few

Philadelphia Fleabane
Erigeron philadelphicus

This pretty native wildflower is usually considered a weed to be pulled on sight in gardens and along sidewalks. However, if left to grow, Philadelphia fleabane will produce lovely flowerheads—each ringed with more than 100 slender florets—from late spring to autumn. • In the early 1900s, physicians used oils from the leaves and flower clusters of this plant to speed up contractions and to stop bleeding during births. Philadelphia fleabane has also been used to control nosebleeds and internal bleeding and to treat fevers, coughs, diabetes and even tumours. • The smoke produced by burning some *Erigeron* species was used to drive away fleas and other insect pests, giving rise to the common name fleabane.

Plant: soft-hairy biennial or perennial 15–90 cm tall, from rootstock and runners
Leaves: blunt-toothed to lobed, 5–15 cm long; lower leaves short-stalked, stem leaves stalkless and clasping
Flowerheads: rose purple to white, 1–2.5 cm across, with 100–400 slender strap-like florets around a yellow button of tubular florets; flowerheads in branched clusters **Blooms:** April to August
Fruits: seed-like achenes tipped with a tuft of white hairs **Habitat:** various; usually disturbed sites **Distribution:** native from Newfoundland to the Yukon to Texas **Pick:** a few

Spotted Joe-Pye Weed
Eupatorium maculatum

Joe Pye, a 19th-century European, promoted the lifestyle of North American Native peoples and used this plant to cure fevers during a typhus outbreak in New England. Traditionally, the root of Joe-Pye weed was used to increase sweating and urination and to generally cleanse the system, so it was included in treatments for various illnesses, including diabetes, rheumatism and persistent kidney and bladder problems. The dried plants have a vanilla-like fragrance and are said to make a pleasant tea. • Spotted Joe-Pye weed plants try to capture as much light as possible. Each ring of leaves is staggered so the blades line up with spaces between the leaves below. • *E. maculatum* has also been called *E. purpureum* var. *maculatum*.

Plant: erect perennial 60–200 cm tall, with hollow, purplish stems **Leaves:** in circles (whorls) of 3–5; lance-shaped, 6–20 cm long, coarsely sharp-toothed, short-stalked **Flowerheads:** fuzzy, pinkish purple to pale lavender, about 8 mm across, with 9–22 tubular florets above overlapping rows of 3–5-nerved bracts; flowerheads in flat-topped, 10–14 cm wide clusters **Blooms:** July to September **Fruits:** seed-like achenes with a tuft of soft hairs **Habitat:** moist, open sites **Distribution:** native from Newfoundland to B.C. to New Mexico; rare in Alberta, Montana and a few southeastern states **Pick:** a few

Leafy Spurge
Euphorbia esula

This aggressive weed appeared in Ontario in 1889. Forty years later it had spread to British Columbia, and within a century more than 1 million hectares were infested in North America. With their exploding capsules, leafy spurge plants can shoot seeds up to 5 m away. Seeds also float along streams to establish new colonies. To make matters worse, tiny pieces of the deep, easily broken roots can grow into new plants, and the decaying leaves poison livestock (although sheep seem to be immune). Leafy spurge quickly displaces native plants and reduces rangeland productivity by 50–75%.
• The name *Euphorbia* honours Euphorbus, physician to a king of Mauritania in the first century BC.
• Take care! The milky juice can burn sensitive skin and may cause blindness if it touches the eyes.

Plant: hairless perennial 30–70 cm tall, from strong, spreading roots **Leaves:** slender, 3–8 cm long, stalkless **Flowers:** tiny, in 2 mm wide groups resembling single flowers; each group has 4 male flowers and 1 stalked female flower in a cup with 4 crescent-shaped glands above 2 petal-like bracts; flower groups in branched, umbrella-shaped clusters with circles (whorls) of leaves at the main base and paired, heart-shaped bracts below smaller sub-clusters **Blooms:** June to August **Fruits:** 3–3.5 mm capsules **Habitat:** disturbed sites **Distribution:** Eurasia; naturalized across temperate North America **Pick:** freely; caution

Queen Anne's Lace
Daucus carota

This lacy wildflower is the great-grandmother of domestic carrots. When carrots from the gardens of early settlers began to grow wild, their offspring changed back to the form of their ancestor, Queen Anne's lace, and then spread across the country. One plant can produce up to 40,000 barbed seeds, which are cupped in clusters resembling bird's nests. • The first-year roots of wild plants smell and taste like garden carrots, but they are white, smaller, less crisp and more fragrant. Like carrots, they can be eaten raw or cooked. The young leaves and flower clusters are also edible raw or cooked, and seeds that are just mature make an aromatic spice for tea, yogurt and fruit salad. Younger and older seeds, however, have an unpleasant flavour.

Plant: erect biennial 40–100 cm tall, from stout taproot **Leaves:** 5–20 cm long, repeatedly pinnately divided into slender leaflets **Flowers:** tiny, white to creamy (the central flower sometimes purple to reddish brown); many flowers grouped in lacy, umbrella-shaped, 4–12 cm wide clusters with spreading, finely divided bracts at base **Blooms:** June to September **Fruits:** bristly, seed-like, 3–4 mm schizocarps **Habitat:** disturbed sites **Distribution:** Eurasia; naturalized across temperate Canada (except the prairies), south through the U.S. **Pick:** freely

Wild Parsnip
Pastinaca sativa

Early settlers brought parsnips to North America as a source of food, fodder and medicine. Although wild parsnip roots are thinner and more aromatic than those of their home-grown relatives, they can still be gathered at the end of the first growing season and used as a sweet, starchy vegetable. Creative Irish cottagers used parsnips to make beer, wine and a marmalade-like preserve. The young shoots are also edible, but older leaves soon become too strong-flavoured. The strong-smelling, oil-rich fruits have been used as a spice. In Britain, parsnips were considered excellent livestock feed, especially good for fattening pigs. • People with sensitive skin can develop rashes if they touch parsnip plants and then go out into bright sunlight.

Plant: erect biennial 60–150 cm tall, with sturdy, grooved stems from a stout taproot **Leaves:** pinnately divided into 5–15 large (5–10 cm long), toothed and lobed leaflets **Flowers:** tiny, yellow; many borne in 5–20 cm wide, umbrella-shaped clusters with 15–25 main branches; clusters usually lacking bracts at the base **Blooms:** June to September **Fruits:** flattened, winged, seed-like schizocarps 5–7 mm long **Habitat:** disturbed ground **Distribution:** Eurasia; naturalized across most of North America **Pick:** freely; caution

Common Cow-Parsnip
Heracleum maximum

Although mature cow-parsnip is strong-smelling, many tribes used it for food. Young shoots and stems were peeled, then cooked or eaten raw, often dipped in grease or sugar. Sometimes stalks were roasted in coals and then peeled. The aromatic seeds flavoured soups and stews, and the ashes of burned leaves became a kind of salt. Some people liken the roots to rutabagas, but others find the taste too strong to be enjoyable. • The dried, hollow stems can be used to make elk and moose whistles, children's flutes, drinking straws and toy blowguns, but these items may irritate the lips. People with sensitive skin often develop rashes when contact with cow-parsnip is followed by exposure to bright sunlight. It is best to gather this robust plant with gloves.

Plant: hairy perennial 1–3 m tall, with hollow stems **Leaves:** divided into 3 large (10–30 cm), lobed, toothed leaflets; upper leaf stalks with enlarged bases **Flowers:** small, white; many in twice-divided, umbrella-like clusters 10–20 cm wide with 15–30 main branches **Blooms:** June to July **Fruits:** flattened, heart-shaped, seed-like schizocarps 8–12 mm long **Habitat:** moist, rich sites **Distribution:** native across North America and in Siberia **Pick:** a few

Common Water-Parsnip
Sium suave

S ome tribes believed that smoke from common water-parsnip seeds could drive away evil spirits trying to steal a hunter's luck. The slender, fleshy, nutty-flavoured roots were harvested in early spring and eaten raw or cooked. The leaves are also said to be edible but very strong-tasting. However, water-parsnip is so similar to its highly poisonous relatives (such as spotted water-hemlock, p. 86), it is better left alone. Reports of poisoning most likely come from confusion with toxic species. Water-parsnip has ribbed stems and a circle (whorl) of small bracts at the base of each of its flower clusters, whereas water-hemlock has smooth, rounded stalks and lacks bracts. Unfortunately, by the time a water-parsnip plant is large enough identify with certainty, its roots are too woody to eat.

Plant: erect perennial 60–200 cm tall, from fibrous roots **Leaves:** pinnately divided into 7–17 narrow, 5–10 cm long, sharply toothed leaflets **Flowers:** tiny, white; many in flat-topped, 3–12 cm wide, umbrella-shaped clusters with 6–20 main branches above a ring of 5–8 slender bracts **Blooms:** July to September **Fruits:** oval, corky-ribbed, seed-like schizocarps 2–3 mm long **Habitat:** wet, open sites **Distribution:** native from Newfoundland to Alaska to the southern U.S. and in Siberia **Pick:** none

Spotted Water-Hemlock
Cicuta maculata

Spotted water-hemlock is one of our most poisonous wild plants: a single rootstock can kill a horse. Children have been poisoned by using peashooters made from water-hemlock stems. Symptoms include stomach pains, vomiting, weak and rapid pulse and convulsions. If you know someone may have eaten any part of a water-hemlock plant, take a sample and get medical help immediately. • Spotted water-hemlock has swollen, chambered rootstocks and yellowish, oily, foul-smelling sap. The main side-veins of the leaves end at the bases of the leaf teeth, not at the tooth tips. Remember: 'Vein to the cut, pain in the gut!' • A similar European species, poison-hemlock *(Conium maculatum)*, was the plant used to kill Socrates. It now grows wild in Ontario. Watch for its purple-blotched stems and finely divided leaves.

Plant: erect perennial 60–200 cm tall, with ridged, thick-based stems from fibrous roots **Leaves:** 2–3 times pinnately divided into sharply toothed, 3–10 cm long leaflets **Flowers:** tiny, white; many in 5–12 cm wide, umbrella-shaped clusters, usually without bracts at the base **Blooms:** June to August **Fruits:** round, slightly flattened, corky-ribbed, seed-like schizocarps 2–4 mm long **Habitat:** wet sites **Distribution:** native from Nova Scotia to Alaska to Mexico **Pick:** none (abundant, but toxic)

Northern Bedstraw

Galium boreale

This herb belongs to the same family as coffee, and its tiny nutlets can be roasted as a coffee substitute. The name bedstraw refers to the historical use of European plants as a fragrant stuffing for mattresses and pillows. Young plants are edible, but more often bedstraw has been used as medicine, often in hot poultices to stop bleeding and reduce swelling. The plant juice has been applied alone or in salves to heal sunburn, rashes, cuts, insect bites, eczema, ringworm and other skin problems. Northern bedstraw tea was traditionally taken to relieve diarrhea, bladder infections and kidney stones, but more recently it has been promoted as a weight-loss aid. Continued use, however, can irritate the mouth and tongue.

Plant: erect, leafy perennial 20–80 cm tall, with simple or branched, smooth, 4-angled stems
Leaves: in circles (whorls) of 4; narrow, 3-nerved, 1.5–4.5 cm long, stalkless **Flowers:** white or creamy, 3.5–7 mm across, with 4 spreading petal lobes; many flowers in showy, branched clusters
Blooms: June to August **Fruits:** pairs of seed-like nutlets, 2 mm long **Habitat:** variable, but not too dry **Distribution:** native from Quebec to Alaska and around the world **Pick:** a few

Hoary Alyssum
Berteroa incana

This delicate wildflower has become a widespread weed in eastern North America, sometimes forming a lacy blanket of dainty white blooms. It has been planted occasionally as an ornamental. Hoary alyssum thrives in dry, sandy areas and will often become abundant in pastures after drought or winterkill. Although it is not usually considered a problem species for ruminants, such as cattle and sheep, it can be toxic for horses. Some horses develop depression, leg swelling, fever and diarrhea and even founder after eating hay or forage containing large amounts of this plant. • Hoary alyssum is also known as hoary false madwort and hoary alison. The name *Berteroa* honours C.G.L. Bertero (1789–1831), an Italian botanist.

Plant: leafy-stemmed annual, biennial or perennial up to 70 cm tall, greyish from dense, star-shaped hairs **Leaves:** lance-shaped, 2–5 cm long, smooth-edged, short-stalked to stalkless **Flowers:** white, 3 mm wide, cross-shaped, with 4 deeply 2-lobed petals and 4 sepals; flowers in elongating clusters **Blooms:** June to September **Fruits:** plump, elliptic capsules 5–8 mm long, tipped with a persistent style; containing 6–12 seeds **Habitat:** disturbed ground **Distribution:** Europe; naturalized across temperate North America **Pick:** freely

Curly Dock
Rumex crispus

Tart, lemony dock leaves make a flavourful addition to stews, soups and stir-fries, but they can become quite bitter with age. In moderation, the tender young leaves add zing to salads and sandwiches. Like its cousin common rhubarb *(Rheum rhabarbarum)*, curly dock contains oxalic acid, which is toxic in large quantities. The seeds are edible and were pounded into meal or roasted as a coffee substitute. The fleshy winter roots were collected during spring plowing and cooked as a vegetable. Some herbalists use dock as a liver stimulant, blood cleanser and mild laxative. • This prolific immigrant is a naturalized weed around the world. Each plant can produce more than 60,000 seeds that can survive for up to 80 years.

Plant: erect perennial 50–150 cm tall, from taproot **Leaves:** lance-shaped, 10–30 cm long, with finely rippled edges and rounded to notched bases
Flowers: green or pinkish, with 3 tiny sepals and 3 larger inner flaps (valves); flowers in circles (whorls) in narrow, branched, 10–40 cm long clusters
Blooms: April to July **Fruits:** 3-sided, seed-like achenes enclosed by 3 papery, golden to red-brown, 5 mm long valves each with a conspicuous wart-like bump
Habitat: moist, often disturbed sites
Distribution: Eurasia; naturalized across Canada and the U.S. **Pick:** freely

Tall Meadowrue
Thalictrum dasycarpum

Tall meadowrue produces blooms in abundance. Although the flowers are small and lack petals, they form conspicuous, showy clusters on tall stems. Each plant is either male or female. The males are easily recognized by their clusters of dangling stamens, whereas the females are less showy at first but develop distinctive heads of small fruits later in summer. • In the first century AD, Pliny recommended meadowrue for preventing baldness and restoring hair. Since then, these plants have seldom been used as medicine. Most species, however, produce chemicals called alkaloids, some of which have been used to combat tumours. A few species contain the heart toxin thalictrine. • Meadowrue seeds and leaves remain fragrant when dried and make a nice addition to sachets for scenting clothing drawers and linen cupboards.

Plant: leafy, often purplish perennial 1–2 m tall **Leaves:** 3–4 times divided in threes; leaflets 3-lobed **Flowers:** pale yellow to purplish, with 4–5 slender sepals (no petals), male and female flowers usually on separate plants in leafy, pyramid-shaped clusters; anthers 1.5–3.5 mm long **Blooms:** June to July **Fruits:** 6–8-ribbed, seed-like achenes, 4–6 mm long, in hemispherical heads **Habitat:** wet, open sites **Distribution:** native from Ontario to Alberta, south to Missouri and Oklahoma **Pick:** a few

Pickerelweed

Pontederia cordata

This beautiful aquatic plant, with its striking blue flowers, is sometimes grown as an ornamental in European water gardens. Unlike its infamous relative, the pestilential water-hyacinth *(Eichornia crassipes)*, our native pickerelweed is a welcome resident of local waterways. • Pickerelweed has often been used for food. Each fruit contains a nutritious, starchy seed that can be eaten straight from the plant or dried and added to granola and other cereals. The dried seeds can also be boiled, roasted to improve flavour or ground into flour. The young leaves (not fully unfurled) have sometimes been eaten raw in salads or boiled and served with butter.

Plant: aquatic perennial up to 100 cm tall, from creeping buried stems **Leaves:** firm, broadly heart-shaped to lance-shaped, up to 18 cm long, long-stalked **Flowers:** violet blue (rarely white), funnel-shaped, 2-lipped; borne in crowded, 5–15 cm long spikes above a loose, 3–6 cm, sheathing bract (spathe) **Blooms:** June to October **Fruits:** beaked, seed-like, 5–10 mm capsules inside enlarged tubes of fused sepals **Habitat:** shallow water **Distribution:** native from Nova Scotia to Ontario, south to South America **Pick:** none

Buckbean
Menyanthes trifoliata

In Europe, powdered buckbean roots were mixed with flour as a nutritious but bitter-tasting bread additive. This practice was especially common in times of famine. More commonly, the bitter leaves were used as a substitute for hops in flavouring beer and were also boiled in honey to make mead. Through the years, buckbean has been used to treat many ailments, including jaundice, indigestion, skin diseases, scurvy, intestinal worms and rheumatism. None of these uses has been proved effective, though the strong-tasting bitters may help to stimulate appetite. Some people recommend buckbean leaf as a pleasantly bitter addition to summer salads and cream-cheese sandwiches, but only in small amounts. Larger servings cause vomiting and diarrhea.

Plant: fleshy, hairless perennial 10–30 cm tall, from coarse rootstock **Leaves:** basal, long-stalked, divided into 3 leaflets 3–8 cm long, with smooth or wavy edges **Flowers:** white, usually purple-tinged, funnel-shaped, about 2 cm across, with 5 spreading, hairy petals; 10–20 flowers in elongated clusters held just above the water **Blooms:** May to July **Fruits:** thick-walled, egg-shaped capsules, 6–9 mm long **Habitat:** standing water **Distribution:** native from Newfoundland to Alaska to the southwestern U.S. and around the world **Pick:** none

Wapato
Sagittaria latifolia

The starchy winter tubers of wapato have been likened to potatoes in texture and chestnuts in flavour. Patient Native women worked in chest-deep, ice-cold water to gather these delicious gems. By hanging from a small canoe, women could dislodge roots with their toes and scoop tubers that bobbed to the surface. Wapato tubers could be eaten raw, but usually they were boiled, steamed or baked in coals. Ducks, swans and muskrats also relish these nutritious roots, and people sometimes raided muskrat push-ups (lodges) to steal their caches.
• 'Wapato' may be a contraction of 'water potato.' This plant has also been called duck potato and arrowhead. The scientific name literally translates as 'broad-leaved arrowhead.'

Plant: variable aquatic perennial 30–120 cm tall, with large (up to 5 cm) tuberous roots on spreading underground stems
Leaves: basal, arrowhead-shaped, occasionally unlobed, 5–40 cm long
Flowers: white, 1.5–3 cm across, with 3 petals; flowers in circles (whorls) of 3, forming elongated clusters with female flowers at the base and male flowers at the top **Blooms:** July to September
Fruits: dry, seed-like achenes, tipped with a 0.6–1.8 mm beak and edged with wings
Habitat: wet ground or calm, shallow water **Distribution:** native across Canada and south to tropical America
Pick: none

Starry False Solomon's-Seal
Maianthemum stellatum

This graceful wildflower is named for its delicate, star-shaped flowers. 'Solomon's-seal' refers to a six-pointed star like the Star of David, and *stellatum* means 'star-like.' Although the berries can taste sweet, large amounts cause vomiting and diarrhea when eaten raw. The rootstocks were sometimes used for food, but usually they had to be soaked in lye to remove their bitterness, then washed and boiled to remove the lye. Like onions, these fleshy roots were used to flavour other foods. Medicinally, the roots were chewed raw or used in syrups and teas to relieve coughs. They were also applied as poultices to burns and swellings. The young leaves and shoots are edible, but this lovely plant should be gathered only in an emergency. • This species has also been called *Smilacina stellata*.

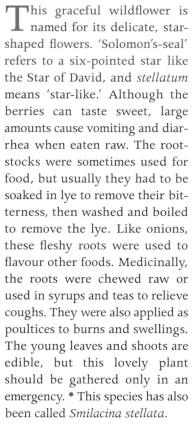

Plant: erect perennial 20–60 cm tall, from rootstock **Leaves:** alternate on zigzagged stems, oblong to lance-shaped, 6–15 cm long, usually folded, sometimes clasping **Flowers:** white, 8–10 mm across, with 6 oblong tepals; flowers in elongated, 2–5 cm clusters **Blooms:** May to June **Fruits:** 6–10 mm berries, green with 6 dark stripes at first, blackish red when mature **Habitat:** moist woods, shores and meadows **Distribution:** native from Newfoundland to Alaska, south through the U.S. **Pick:** none

White Death-Camas
Zigadenus elegans

Beware! All parts of this rather innocent-looking wildflower contain toxic chemicals (alkaloids) said to be more potent than strychnine. Sheep (especially), cattle, horses and even chickens have been poisoned by death-camas, with losses of up to 2000 animals at a time. Human deaths have usually occurred when the bulbs were mistaken for those of wild onion (*Allium* spp.) or camas (*Camassia* spp). Just two bulbs can be fatal. Symptoms include salivating, vomiting, diarrhea, lowered body temperature and a slow heartbeat. If you think that someone has eaten these bulbs, encourage vomiting and get the person to a doctor as soon as possible. • *Zigadenus* means 'paired glands,' referring to the two-lobed gland on each petal.

Plant: erect perennial 20–60 cm tall, from an onion-like bulb **Leaves:** grass-like, blue-green, mostly basal, up to 1.2 cm wide, with parallel veins **Flowers:** white to greenish white, star-shaped, with 6 oblong, 7–12 mm long tepals each bearing a green, heart-shaped gland near the base; flowers in branched clusters 10–30 cm long **Blooms:** July to August **Fruits:** egg-shaped, 1–1.5 cm long capsules containing angular, 3 mm seeds **Habitat:** moist to wet, open sites **Distribution:** native from Quebec to Alaska, south to Mexico **Pick:** none (abundant, but toxic)

Snow Trillium
Trillium grandiflorum

Patient gardeners may plant Ontario's beautiful floral emblem in shady nooks, but trilliums must grow for at least six years before they flower. As the fruits mature, they bend close to the ground and split open, exposing clumps of sticky seeds. Each seed has a large bump, called an elaiosome, that ants find irresistible. When ants carry trillium seeds back to their nest, the elaiosome is eaten and the seed discarded (planted) well away from the parent plant. • Some Native peoples used snow trillium roots and rootstocks as medicine, and the young leaves are said to make excellent salad and cooked greens, but it would be a shame to kill such a beautiful plant.

Plant: erect perennial 20–40 cm tall, from short rootstock **Leaves:** 3 in a circle (whorl), ovate to rounded, 8–15 cm long, stalkless **Flowers:** waxy-white (pink with age), 5–10 cm across, with 3 showy petals, 3 smaller green sepals, 6 stamens and a white, 6-winged ovary; flowers solitary above the leaves on erect, 5–8 cm stalks **Blooms:** April to June **Fruits:** many-seeded red berries **Habitat:** rich woods **Distribution:** native in Quebec, Ontario and the eastern U.S. **Pick:** none

Wood Lily
Lilium philadelphicum

This bright orange wildflower creates splashes of colour along waysides across Canada. It is Saskatchewan's floral emblem. • Many tribes gathered the bulbs of wood lily for food and medicine. The bulbs are said to have an excellent flavour, either raw or cooked. As well, the abundant, nutritious pollen can be dusted on various dishes. Medicinally, the bulbs were once cooked and then applied to sores, bruises, swellings or wounds. They were also used to make a medicinal tea for treating stomach problems, coughs and fevers and for helping women in labour deliver the afterbirth. • Wood lilies have disappeared from many populated areas. Picking the flowers with their leafy stems or gathering the roots kills these beautiful plants. Please leave them for others to enjoy.

Plant: erect perennial 30–90 cm tall, from 2–3 cm thick bulb **Leaves:** slender, 3–10 cm long, rough-edged, in circles (whorls) of 3–8 upwards on the stem, often alternate below **Flowers:** usually reddish orange (red to yellowish), with 6 purple-spotted tepals, broadly funnel-shaped, 6–10 cm long, held erect; 1–5 flowers per plant **Blooms:** June to August **Fruits:** oblong capsules 4–7 cm long, with packed rows of flat seeds **Habitat:** dry woods, meadows, roadsides **Distribution:** native from Quebec to B.C., south to New Mexico **Pick:** none

Orange Daylily
Hemerocallis fulva

For thousands of years, fields of this lovely lily have been grown for food in China and Japan. The flower buds, eaten raw, pickled or slightly steamed, are said to resemble green beans in taste and texture. The opened flowers add zest and colour to salads, but they can also be fried or added to soups as an aromatic thickener. The tuberous root-stocks provide a crisp vegetable similar to water chestnuts, though older ones must be cooked. The young shoots and leaves are also edible raw. • The names *Hemerocallis* and daylily both mean 'beautiful for a day,' because each blossom lasts for only 1 day. • More than 12,000 garden varieties of daylilies have been developed, with hundreds more added yearly. These popular perennials thrive in almost any soil.

Plant: erect perennial 60–120 cm tall, from thick, spreading rootstock **Leaves:** many, basal, sword-like, channelled, 60–90 cm long **Flowers:** tawny orange, funnel-shaped, about 9–12 cm across, with 6 spreading tepals (the petals are wavy-edged), 6 stamens and a style with a cap-like stigma; 6–15 flowers in loose, branched clusters **Blooms:** June to August **Fruits:** oblong, 3-sided capsules **Habitat:** meadows, streambanks, road-sides **Distribution:** Eurasia; naturalized in the eastern U.S. and Canada and in some western states **Pick:** freely

Northern Blue Flag
Iris versicolor

This beautiful flower, with its colourful, arching petals, was named in honour of *Iris* (meaning 'rainbow'), a messenger of the Greek gods responsible for transporting women's souls to paradise. Through the years, iris flowers have symbolized power, with the three parts representing wisdom, faith and courage. • Irises have been used medicinally in the past, but their rootstocks are dangerously poisonous. Some tribes used the two outermost fibres of the leaves to spin strong, very fine, highly esteemed twine. Today, northern blue flag is popular with gardeners as a showy flower for brightening wet sites. • Powdered iris root, called orris, smells like violets and has been added to perfume and potpourri.

Plant: erect or arching perennial 20–80 cm tall, from creeping rootstock
Leaves: greyish green, sword-shaped, 1.3–2.5 cm wide **Flowers:** violet blue to reddish purple (rarely white), purple-veined, 6–8 cm across, with 3 broad, petal-like sepals below 3 smaller, erect petals and 3 petal-like, 2-lobed styles; 1 to several flowers in elongating clusters
Blooms: May to July **Fruits:** erect, 3-sided capsules, 3.5–6 cm long, containing rows of pebbled seeds **Habitat:** wet sites **Distribution:** native from Newfoundland to Manitoba, south to Virginia and Minnesota **Pick:** none

Common Blue-Eyed-Grass
Sisyrinchium montanum

The cheerful blue eyes of this dainty wildflower often seem to float among blades of grass. Without the sun, the flower petals close, and this slender plant disappears among its grassy neighbours. • Common blue-eyed-grass is not a grass at all. It belongs to the iris family, a group with showy, brightly coloured flowers. Try running your fingers along the stems. You'll discover that they are distinctly two-sided, not round like those of grass. • A few tribes added this plant to medicinal teas for diarrhea, worms and stomachaches, but common blue-eyed-grass has not been widely used. The seeds can take more than two years to germinate, so these delicate blue blooms seldom peek out from flowerbeds.

Plant: slender, clumped perennial 10–50 cm tall, with unbranched, flattened, narrow-winged stems 1–4 mm wide
Leaves: grass-like, 1–3.5 mm wide
Flowers: bright violet blue, star-shaped, 6–10 mm across, with 6 abruptly pointed or notched tepals; flowers single or in small clusters from between two 1–6 cm bracts at stem tips **Blooms:** late May to July **Fruits:** round, 3–6 mm capsules on thread-like stalks **Habitat:** moist, open sites **Distribution:** native from New-foundland to the Yukon, south to North Carolina and Texas **Pick:** a few

White Water-Lily
Nymphaea odorata

This beautiful, hardy plant is easy to grow and is ideal for garden pools.
Each day for 4–5 days, the showy, fragrant flowers open early in the morning and close by early afternoon. Once a flower has been pollinated, its stem
coils like a spring and pulls the developing fruit underwater. Over the next 3–4
weeks, the seeds develop inside a fleshy berry. When it finally matures, the
fruit breaks free and bobs to the surface. The large, floating berry then gradually rots, shedding its 600–700 small, green seeds around the pond. • The
starchy seeds of various water-lilies are used for food around the world. They
are ground into flour, boiled in water and even cooked in hot sand.

Plant: aquatic perennial **Leaves:** floating,
round with a V-shaped notch, 10–30 cm
long, shiny green, often purplish underneath
Flowers: white (rarely pinkish), single,
7–20 cm across, with many white petals,
4 green sepals and 40–100 stamens around
a disc (stigma) with 10 to 25 lines radiating
from the centre **Blooms:** June to September **Fruits:** egg-shaped, spongy to leathery
berries surrounded by incurved sepals
Habitat: quiet water **Distribution:**
native across Canada (except Alberta),
south through the U.S. **Pick:** none

Yellow Pond-Lily
Nuphar lutea

Long, slender stalks anchor these floating flowers and leaves to deeply buried rootstocks. The stalks contain large air-filled tubes that carry oxygen to the roots and waste gases to the surface. Native peoples gathered the thick rootstocks in winter and spring, boiled or roasted them for several hours, then peeled them to expose their sweet, gluey contents. Rootstocks were also sliced, dried and ground into meal or flour. The starchy seeds can be difficult to remove, so some tribes rotted the fruits until the pods became soft. The heated seeds swell like poor-quality popcorn, making a crunchy snack. • This species includes *N. variegata*.

Plant: aquatic perennial from large rootstock
Leaves: floating (sometimes underwater), round-heart-shaped, 7–35 cm long, on long, narrowly winged stalks **Flowers:** single, cupped, 3.5–6 cm across, with about 6 yellow, petal-like sepals (often reddish inside) and many large (4–7 mm) anthers around a yellowish, 1 cm disc (stigma) with about 10–15 lines radiating from the centre **Blooms:** May to September **Fruits:** egg-shaped, spongy to leathery berries, 2–4.5 cm long **Habitat:** quiet waters **Distribution:** native across North America **Pick:** none

Yellow Marsh-Marigold
Caltha palustris

Bright yellow clumps of this shining flower brighten many dark, damp hollows in spring and early summer. Although the buttercup-like blooms appear evenly yellow to human eyes, their petal tips reflect ultraviolet light and their bases absorb it. As a result, insects such as bees, whose eyes detect ultraviolet light, see distinct patterns that direct them to nectaries at the centre of the flower. • Yellow marsh-marigold is sometimes grown as an ornamental in moist, shady gardens. This rather toxic plant has also been used for food and medicine, but it contains strong irritants that can cause blistering, and it is poisonous if eaten raw.

Plant: fleshy perennial 20–60 cm tall, with thick, hollow stems **Leaves:** dark green, heart-shaped to kidney-shaped, 5–17 cm long, shallowly toothed, smaller and more widely notched upwards on the stem **Flowers:** bright, shiny yellow, saucer-shaped, 1.5–4 cm across, with 5–9 petal-like sepals (no petals), 50–120 stamens and a dense cluster of pistils; flowers in branched clusters **Blooms:** April to June **Fruits:** capsules (follicles) 1–1.5 cm long, borne in head-like clusters **Habitat:** wet sites, often in shallow water **Distribution:** native across North America and around the world **Pick:** none; caution

Meadow Buttercup
Ranunculus acris

Some sources suggest meadow buttercup as a lovely addition to the garden, but unsuspecting gardeners will likely find themselves fighting to keep this prolific European weed at bay. • The specific epithet *acris* refers to the acrid sap of this buttercup. The caustic, bitter juice discourages browsers, but it can also blister sensitive skin. • The characteristic shininess of these flowers comes from a specialized film of white cells in the petals that reflects light. Tall stems hold the bright yellow blooms above surrounding plants to attract the attention of pollinating insects.

Plant: slender, branched perennial 60–100 cm tall **Leaves:** kidney-shaped, divided into wedge-shaped, deeply lobed parts arranged like fingers on a hand (palmate) **Flowers:** glossy yellow, saucer-shaped, about 2.5 cm across, with 5 broadly ovate petals, 5 greenish, spreading sepals and many stamens and pistils; few to several flowers in loose clusters **Blooms:** May to September **Fruits:** flattened, seed-like achenes, 2–3 mm long, with a 0.4–1 mm beak; achenes in round heads **Habitat:** meadows and disturbed habitats **Distribution:** Europe; naturalized across North America **Pick:** freely; caution

Canada Anemone
Anemone canadensis

This common wildflower is easily identified by the circle of coarsely toothed, stalkless leaves high on its flower stems. Anemone flowers have no true petals. Instead, the five showy sepals attract pollinating insects. • In the western U.S., some tribes attributed mystical powers to Canada anemone and valued its roots as medicine, applied in washes and poultices. However, anemones contain many of the caustic substances that are common in species of the buttercup family, so handle these plants with care, especially if you have sensitive skin. • Another common name for anemone is windflower. The genus name comes from the Greek *anemos,* 'wind,' because these beautiful flowers were thought to open with the first breezes of spring.

Plant: erect perennial 20–80 cm tall, from spreading rootstock **Leaves:** cut into 3–5 sharply toothed parts, long-stalked at the plant base and stalkless in a circle below the flowers **Flowers:** white, saucer-shaped, 2.5–3.8 cm across, with 5 petal-like sepals (no petals); flowers single or 2–3 **Blooms:** May to August **Fruits:** seed-like achenes 3–5 mm long, flattened, with flat-lying hairs; achenes in round heads **Habitat:** moist, open sites **Distribution:** native across temperate North America **Pick:** a few; caution

Wild Mustard
Sinapis arvensis

Wild mustard was brought to North America as a source of cooking greens, mustard seasoning and burning oil. Unfortunately, it is now regarded mainly as a noxious weed. A single plant may produce 3500 seeds, which can survive for up to 60 years, germinating when conditions permit. • Many significant crops, including canola and other rapeseed varieties, turnip, cabbage, cauliflower, kale and brown mustard, are species of the genus *Brassica* and are closely related to wild mustard. As a result, wild mustard can be very difficult to identify and control when it invades fields of some of these crops. Not only does wild mustard compete for moisture and nutrients, but its seeds reduce the quality of the oil when mixed with canola. • Wild mustard is also called *Brassica kaber*.

Plant: coarse annual with bristly stems 20–80 cm tall, from slender taproot
Leaves: widest above midleaf, coarsely toothed to lobed, 5–20 cm long
Flowers: yellow, 1.5 cm across, cross-shaped, with 4 petals and 4 sepals; flowers on stout, ascending stalks in elongating clusters **Blooms:** May to July
Fruits: 3- to 5-nerved, cylindrical pods, 1.5–4 cm long, tipped with a 4-sided (sometimes 1-seeded) beak about half as long as the pod **Habitat:** waste places, fields **Distribution:** Eurasia; naturalized across North America **Pick:** freely

Tumbleweed Mustard
Sisymbrium altissimum

This successful immigrant originated in the western Mediterranean region and northern Africa. Early settlers and Native peoples sometimes used its small seeds for seasoning, and a few tribes boiled the ground seed to make gruel. Tumbleweed mustard makes a good potherb, but only when the leaves are young and tender, before the plant blooms. Try adding the young leaves to salads and soups.
• Tumbleweed mustard will occasionally infest fields, but it is not usually considered a noxious weed. A single plant can produce up to 2700 seeds. In fall, the dried skeletons of dead plants form airy spheres that break off near the ground and tumble freely in the wind, scattering seeds along the way and spreading this common weed across the countryside.

Plant: essentially hairless annual (sometimes biennial) 30–100 cm tall, much branched above **Leaves:** stalked, deeply pinnately cut into slender, often toothed lobes; upper leaves skeleton-like **Flowers:** pale yellow, about 6–14 mm across, cross-shaped, with 4 petals and 4 sepals; flowers borne at branch tips in elongating clusters **Blooms:** June to August **Fruits:** slender, ascending to spreading pods, 5–10 cm long, 1–1.5 mm wide, with stalks almost as thick **Habitat:** disturbed ground **Distribution:** Europe; naturalized across North America **Pick:** freely

Sulphur Cinquefoil
Potentilla recta

The small, pale, rose-like flowers of this plant are a relatively recent sight, first reported from North America in 1897. Sulphur cinquefoil has little food value and is seldom eaten by livestock, so in some areas it is one of the most rapidly increasing weeds. • The delicate flowers are short-lived. Those that open in the morning usually shed their petals by late afternoon, and the following day a whole new set of buds opens. Sometimes the ground is strewn with pale yellow, heart-shaped petals. • *Potentilla*, from *potens*, 'potent,' refers to cinquefoils' medicinal powers, especially their ability to stop bleeding and diarrhea in both man and beast.

Plant: erect, hairy perennial 30–80 cm tall
Leaves: mostly basal, green on both sides, divided into 5–7 deeply toothed, 2.5–7.5 cm long leaflets arranged like fingers on a hand (palmate) **Flowers:** sulphur yellow, 1.5–2 cm across, with 5 notched petals above 5 sepals and 5 alternating slender bractlets; flowers in flat-topped clusters **Blooms:** June to August
Fruits: rough-ridged, seed-like achenes, with the style attached at the tip **Habitat:** dry, disturbed sites **Distribution:** Europe; naturalized across Canada and the U.S. **Pick:** freely

Common Silverweed

Argentina anserina

This charming little 'rose' often forms carpets of silver and green leaves dotted with sunny yellow flowers. Although it is easily overlooked, common silverweed is a circumpolar plant with an interesting history. In western Scotland, its starchy roots are said to have saved entire villages from starvation during famines. Raw, boiled or roasted, the spring roots have been likened to parsnips, chestnuts and sweet potatoes. Medicinally, common silverweed was used mainly as an astringent in gargles, washes and teas for reducing inflammation and stopping bleeding of the digestive tract, kidneys and skin. • *A. anserina* has also been called *Potentilla anserina*.

Plant: low perennial with slender, creeping runners **Leaves:** basal, up to 30 cm long, silvery-hairy and woolly underneath, pinnately divided into many sharply toothed leaflets with small and large leaflets interspersed **Flowers:** yellow, 1.5–2.5 cm across, with 5 petals above 5 sepals and 5 smaller, alternating bractlets; flowers single **Blooms:** May to September **Fruits:** thick, furrowed, seed-like achenes, 2.5 mm long, in dense heads **Habitat:** well-drained to wet, open sites **Distribution:** native across North America and around the world **Pick:** a few

Virginia Strawberry

Fragaria virginiana

Although its delicate blooms are easily overlooked, Virginia strawberry is one of our commonest wildflowers. Most people know this little plant for its fruits rather than its flowers. Wild strawberries may be small, but each one packs all the flavour of a larger domestic strawberry. Strawberry-leaf tea provides a refreshing drink that is rich in vitamin C and minerals. For centuries, it has been used as a safe (though not necessarily effective) remedy for everything from insanity to tuberculosis. This tea is still widely used to treat diarrhea and skin problems. If you decide to try strawberry-leaf tea, use only fresh or completely dried leaves, because the wilted leaves contain toxins. Drop in a few strawberries for extra flavour and colour.

Plant: low perennial, often with slender runners
Leaves: basal, long-stalked, with 3 coarsely toothed leaflets each tipped with a relatively small tooth **Flowers:** white, 5-petalled, saucer-shaped, 1.5–2 cm across; in small clusters
Blooms: April to June **Fruits:** strawberries, with tiny, seed-like achenes in pits on the surface of a round, red, fleshy, 1–1.5 cm sphere
Habitat: dry to moist, sunny to shaded, often disturbed sites **Distribution:** throughout North America **Pick:** a few (flowers or fruits)

Bunchberry
Cornus canadensis

Bunchberry makes a lovely groundcover in shady wildflower gardens. Each cheerful little 'flower' is, in fact, a miniature bouquet of tiny blooms surrounded by four showy bracts that look like petals. The bright white bracts lure pollinators to the true flowers, which are so tiny that they are easily overlooked. The bracts also provide landing platforms for insects carrying pollen from other plants. In late summer, dense clusters of small, red berries replace the flowers. Some people enjoy these juicy fruits, with their crunchy little seeds, but others consider them mealy and tasteless. Bunchberries can be eaten as a trail nibble or added to puddings, preserves and sauces.

Plant: colonial perennial 7–20 cm tall, from creeping rootstock **Leaves:** 4–8 cm long, with deep, arched veins; in circles (whorls) of 4–6 at stem tips **Flowers:** tiny, greenish yellow to purplish, clustered at centre of 4 white, petal-like bracts; each flower-like cluster 2–4 cm across **Blooms:** late May to July **Fruits:** red, berry-like drupes, 6–8 mm long, in tight clusters **Habitat:** moist, often acidic sites **Distribution:** native from Newfoundland to Alaska to the northern U.S. and in eastern Asia and Greenland **Pick:** no flowers (fruits in small quantities)

Cultivated Flax
Linum usitatissimum

Fields of sparkling blue flowers make flax one of our most beautiful crops. The long, tough stem fibres have been used since prehistoric times to make highly valued linen thread, cord and cloth. Raw or roasted, cultivated flax seeds make a tasty addition to breads and cereals. Ground seeds are best because grinding increases the fibre value and releases valuable oils. Flax oil has been used for centuries to treat coughs, sore throats, burns and skin irritations. Its essential fatty acids lower cholesterol and help relieve arthritic pain and inflammation. Flax oil is also being studied for treating lupus, kidney disease, malaria, breast cancer and colon cancer. This species is well named *usitatissimum*, 'most useful' flax.

Plant: slender, hairless annual 30–90 cm tall, with branched stems from branched, woody rootstock **Leaves:** many, lance-shaped, 3-nerved, 1.5–3.5 cm long **Flowers:** blue (sometimes white), saucer-shaped, about 2.5 cm across, with 5 fragile petals and 7–9 slender sepals (inner ones fringed); flowers in small, branched, open clusters **Blooms:** March to July **Fruits:** round, pointed capsules 6–10 cm long, on erect stalks **Habitat:** disturbed ground **Distribution:** Europe; naturalized throughout North America **Pick:** freely

Musk Mallow
Malva moschata

This showy wildflower makes an attractive, hardy addition to any flower garden, and its tender young roots and shoots are considered excellent salad greens. Older leaves become rather slimy, so they are usually added to soups as a nutritious, okra-like thickener. Musk mallow flower buds, flowers and young green 'cheeses' (button-like fruit clusters) are all edible raw or cooked. Because the mature leaves contain large amounts of mucilage, they have been used for centuries in soothing poultices, cough syrups and laxatives. They are also rich in vitamins A, B_1, B_2 and C and in minerals. • Musk mallow is easily identified by its finely divided leaves and hairy fruits.

Plant: rough-hairy perennial 20–60 cm tall
Leaves: 7.5–10 cm across, divided into 5–7 slender-toothed parts arranged like fingers on a hand (palmate) **Flowers:** pink, white or pale purple, 3.5–5 cm across, with 5 notched, wedge-shaped petals, 5 sepals and 3 slender, sepal-like bracts; stamens fused into a tube tipped with anthers; flowers mostly clustered at stem tips **Blooms:** June to September **Fruits:** densely hairy, 1-seeded; 15–20 arranged like wedges in a wheel of cheese **Habitat:** disturbed ground **Distribution:** Europe; naturalized through much of temperate North America **Pick:** freely

Bouncing Bet

Saponaria officinalis

These plants contain soapy substances called saponins—hence another common name, soapwort, and the scientific name *Saponaria*, from the Latin *sapo*, 'soap.' 'Bouncing Bet' was once a slang term for a washer-woman. Described by Pond (1974) as a 'sturdy, happy plant with an air of practicality,' bouncing Bet was brought to North America by settlers as a source of soap for everything from homemade lace to pewter utensils. All parts of this plant produce an impressive soapy lather. A cup of fresh leaves and 2 cups of water, whirled in a blender, produces a good soap for dishes and fine laundry.

Plant: erect perennial 30–80 cm tall, with swollen stem joints and spreading rootstock
Leaves: paired, 5–10 cm long, pointed, conspicuously 3–5-veined **Flowers:** white to pinkish, about 2.5 cm across, with 5 shallowly notched petals bearing slender appendages at the base and projecting from a tubular, 20-nerved tube of fused sepals; flowers in branched clusters up to 15 cm long **Blooms:** July to September
Fruits: 4-toothed capsules with net-veined seeds **Habitat:** disturbed ground **Distribution:** Eurasia; naturalized across temperate North America and south to Mexico **Pick:** freely

Bladder Campion
Silene vulgaris

Historically, bladder campion saved lives by providing survival food for the people of Minorca when swarms of locusts destroyed the harvest in 1685. The young leaves, with their sweet, pea like flavour, were once popular in Europe as a spring potherb. However, the plant becomes very bitter and unpleasant with age as the soap (saponin) content increases. • Bladder campion is a common weed but not a serious problem in planted fields. It produces exquisite urn-shaped capsules that appear to be made of polished wood. These capsules make an interesting addition to dried-flower arrangements. • *S. vulgaris* has also been called *S. cucubalus*.

Plant: bluish green perennial 20–80 cm tall, from deep roots **Leaves:** paired, ovate, 3–10 cm long, often clasping, sometimes fringed **Flowers:** whitish, with 5 white, deeply 2-lobed, 3.5–6 mm wide petal blades sticking out from a papery, grey-green to purple-tinged balloon of fused sepals about 1 cm across; flowers in clusters of 5–30 **Blooms:** April to August **Fruits:** 3-chambered capsules opening by 6 teeth, enclosed in sepal balloons 1–2 cm across **Habitat:** disturbed ground **Distribution:** Europe; naturalized across North America **Pick:** freely

Common St. John's-Wort
Hypericum perforatum

Beauty is in the eye of the beholder. Common St. John's-wort can be seen as a nasty weed or as a useful medicinal herb. Few animals eat the acrid foliage, so this hardy immigrant can spread rapidly, choking out valuable forage plants. In California alone, more than 800,000 hectares became infested from 1900 to 1951. • Medicinally, St. John's-wort flower extracts have been used to heal cuts, sores and bruises, and the deep red leaf oil is used in lotions for wounds, burns and rheumatic joints. Dark dots on the leaves and flowers contain hypericin, an antidepressant, used for treating everything from irritability and insomnia to cramps, congestion, bladder problems and worms. It is now being studied as a drug for viral infections.

Plant: leafy perennial with tough, branched stems 30–80 cm tall **Leaves:** paired, oblong, 1–4 cm long, with translucent dots **Flowers:** yellow, about 2 cm across, with 5 showy petals edged with black dots, 5 slender sepals, many stamens (arranged in 3 bundles) and 3 styles; flowers in branched, flat-topped or rounded clusters **Blooms:** June to September **Fruits:** egg-shaped capsules 7–8 mm long **Habitat:** disturbed sites **Distribution:** Europe; naturalized in eastern Canada, B.C. and across the U.S. **Pick:** freely

Purple Loosestrife
Lythrum salicaria

Purple loosestrife was introduced to North America in the 1800s as a showy, hardy, disease-resistant garden flower. Today, its brilliant purplish pink flowers smother wetlands across the continent. The garden varieties were thought sterile (incapable of producing seed), but they soon proved to be decidedly otherwise. One plant can produce more than 2,000,000 seeds, and plants also grow quickly from creeping rootstocks and from root or stem fragments. This aggressive weed has been called 'the silent killer' because few local animals can eat its acrid leaves, tiny seeds and tough roots. Consequently, purple loosestrife thrives unmolested, rapidly choking out native plants and converting complex wetland ecosystems into silent monocultures that are largely unpopulated by insects, birds and frogs.

Plant: stout perennial 50–150 cm tall, from spreading rootstock **Leaves:** paired or in threes, 3–10 cm long, stalkless, sometimes clasping the stem **Flowers:** red-purple, 1–2 cm across, usually with 6 wrinkled petals, 6 sepals (sometimes 4) and twice as many, alternately long and short stamens; many flowers in leafy-bracted, branched, spike-like clusters 10–40 cm long **Blooms:** July to August **Fruits:** small capsules **Habitat:** wet sites **Distribution:** Europe; naturalized across temperate North America **Pick:** freely

Common Fireweed
Chamerion angustifolium

Common fireweed will usually form small colonies along roads, but after fires it can blanket charred landscapes with a sea of rose purple flowers. The sweet blooms provide a tasty nibble, a pretty salad garnish and abundant nectar for golden fireweed honey. Tender young plants (under 20 cm tall) have been likened to asparagus and eaten in the same way. Around the world, people drink fireweed tea and cook the leaves as a potherb. Like any new food, it should be introduced slowly; the uninitiated may find fireweed quite laxative. Older stems have been split lengthwise to scrape out the soft, edible centre (pith) and to prepare the tough stem fibres for making them into twine and fishnets. • *C. angustifolium* is also known by the name *Epilobium angustifolium*.

Plant: erect perennial 50–300 cm tall, from spreading rootstock
Leaves: many, alternate, lance-shaped
Flowers: purplish pink (rarely white), about 2.5 cm across, with 4 slender-based petals, 4 sepals, 8 stamens and a cross-shaped stigma; flowers in spike-like clusters **Blooms:** June to September
Fruits: slender 3–8 cm pods, splitting lengthwise to release tiny seeds with silky parachutes **Habitat:** highly variable, often disturbed **Distribution:** native across North America and around the world **Pick:** a few

Hairy Willowherb
Epilobium hirsutum

This showy Eurasian wild-flower was brought to North America as a garden flower. Its young shoots and leaves are eaten raw or cooked around the world, though Grieve (1931) noted vague reports of toxicity. • The name *Epilobium* comes from the Greek *epi*, 'upon,' and *lobion*, 'small pod,' in reference to the position of the main flower parts (petals, sepals, stamens, style) at the upper tip of a long, thin ovary that eventually becomes a seed pod. A prominent four-lobed stigma projects from each flower, ready to catch pollen carried by visiting insects. If this method fails, the stigma lobes gradually curl back to touch the anthers below, enabling the flower to pollinate itself.

Plant: branched, soft-hairy perennial 50–200 cm tall, from spreading rootstock
Leaves: mostly paired, lance-shaped, sharply toothed, stalkless **Flowers:** rose purple, about 2.5 cm across, with 4 notched, slender-based petals, 4 sepals, 8 stamens and a cross-shaped stigma; flowers in spike-like clusters
Blooms: July to September
Fruits: slender, erect, 5–8 cm pods, splitting lengthwise to release tiny seeds with silky parachutes **Habitat:** moist to wet, often disturbed sites **Distribution:** Eurasia and northern Africa; naturalized in northeastern U.S. and adjacent Canada and in the Pacific Northwest **Pick:** freely

Common Evening-Primrose
Oenothera biennis

Each evening a single delicate flower of common evening-primrose unfurls, releasing its perfume to attract night-flying moths. By noon the following day, the bloom has faded, but if it was pollinated by a moth, its seeds have already started to develop. Each plant usually produces about 6000 oil-rich seeds. North American farmers harvest hundreds of tonnes of evening-primrose seeds each year. The oil from these seeds contains fatty acids that the human body needs in order to produce important hormones. Studies have shown that evening-primrose oil can help treat eczema, asthma, migraine headaches, heart disease, high cholesterol, inflammation, PMS, breast problems, multiple sclerosis, diabetes, rheumatoid arthritis and even alcoholism.

Plant: erect biennial (usually), 50–150 cm tall **Leaves:** lance-shaped to oblong, mostly 10–20 cm long, smooth or wavy-edged **Flowers:** yellow, 2.5–5 cm across, with a long tube (containing the ovary) below 4 petals, 4 sepals, 8 stamens, and a short (less than 2 cm) style tipped with a cross-shaped stigma; flowers in stiff, leafy-bracted spikes **Blooms:** July to September **Fruits:** erect, persistent, oblong capsules, 1.5–4 cm long **Habitat:** disturbed ground **Distribution:** native across southern Canada and most of the U.S. **Pick:** a few

Great Mullein
Verbascum thapsus

Great mullein was introduced to North America in the 1700s as a medicinal herb, and within 100 years, it had spread across the continent. Each plant produces some 150,000 tiny seeds (four fit on the head of a pin). • The large, fuzzy leaves have been used as diapers and toilet paper, but their tiny hairs can irritate sensitive skin. Women sometimes reddened their cheeks by rubbing with mullein leaves. Tall, thick mullein stalks, dipped in melted fat, were burned as torches, and these torches were believed both to repel witches and to be used by them. By a similar contradiction, it was believed that wearing mullein leaves ensured conception, but placing a leaf in one's shoe protected against it.

Plant: stout, grey-woolly biennial 1–2 m tall **Leaves:** thick, felted, up to 30 cm long, in a basal rosette (1st year) and alternate (2nd year), smaller upwards and often with edges extending down the stem **Flowers:** yellow, 1–2.5 cm across, with 5 spreading petal lobes, 5 fuzzy sepals, 5 stamens and 1 style; flowers in dense spikes 20–50 cm long **Blooms:** June to September **Fruits:** 2-parted capsules **Habitat:** disturbed sites **Distribution:** Europe; naturalized from Newfoundland to B.C., Alaska and Texas **Pick:** freely; caution

Fringed Yellow-Loosestrife
Lysimachia ciliata

The name 'loosestrife' suggests that this pretty little wildflower should relieve tension, but instead it often creates confusion. Some say *Lysimachia* came from the Greek *lysis*, or 'loosening,' and *maché*, 'strife,' because it calmed unruly oxen when hung on their yokes. Others believe that it honours the ancient King Lysimachus of Thrace, who discovered its medicinal powers—though it's not clear what those powers are. To add to the confusion, the name *Lysimachia* once referred to both a yellow-flowered plant (now *Lysimachia vulgaris*) and a purple-flowered plant (now *Lythrum salicaria*, p. 117). Plants of both genera have kept the common name 'loosestrife' even though they aren't even distantly related.
• *L. ciliata* is also known by the name *Steironema ciliata*.

Plant: erect perennial 30–130 cm tall, from creeping underground rootstock
Leaves: paired, roughly ovate, 4–14 cm long, with prominently fringed stalks
Flowers: yellow, saucer-shaped, 1.5–2.5 cm across, with 5 abruptly slender-pointed petals, 5 sepals, 5 fertile stamens, 5 sterile stamens and 1 style; flowers borne on slender, 1.5–6.5 cm stalks from leaf axils
Blooms: June to August **Fruits:** small, rounded capsules **Habitat:** moist to wet sites **Distribution:** native from Quebec to B.C., Alaska, southern U.S. **Pick:** a few

Common Milkweed
Asclepias syriaca

Common milkweed colonies produce impressive networks of rope-like runners about 15 cm underground. Each year, a plant can send up dozens of shoots from these runners. • The name milkweed refers to the milky white sap, which contains bitter chemicals to protect the plants from predators. A few lucky insects are immune to these poisons and accumulate them in their bodies, protecting themselves from their own predators. Monarch butterflies cannot complete their life cycles without milkweed. • *Syriaca* means 'of Syria.' Because this milkweed was common in southern Europe, people thought it came from there, but in fact early explorers brought it from North America long before it was officially named.

Plant: perennial 50–150 cm tall, with milky sap **Leaves:** paired, thick, soft-hairy underneath, oblong with rounded bases, 10–20 cm long **Flowers:** 8–12 mm across, with 5 backward-pointing, purplish to greenish petals below a crown of 5 pale purple cups (hoods), each with an upcurved horn; flowers in rounded, umbrella-like clusters **Blooms:** June to August **Fruits:** paired, woolly pods with soft protuberances, 7–12 cm long, releasing silky-parachuted seeds **Habitat:** open, disturbed sites **Distribution:** native from Quebec to Saskatchewan, south through the U.S. **Pick:** freely; caution

Swamp Milkweed
Asclepias incarnata

When insects visit the nectar-rich flowers of swamp milkweed, their feet slip under little saddlebags of pollen, which they have to pull out and carry off when they leave. Occasionally smaller insects cannot free their feet and remain trapped on the flowers. • Although milkweeds are poisonous raw, the young shoots, leaves and seed pods are all edible cooked. When placed in cold water, brought to a boil and simmered till tender (sometimes with a change of water), milkweeds are said to be delicately flavoured and harmless. The flower buds, nectar-sweet flowers and seeds are also edible. • This tall, showy plant adds a beautiful pink accent to wildflower gardens, and like other milkweeds it attracts butterflies.

Plant: erect perennial 30–150 cm tall, with milky sap **Leaves:** paired, lance-shaped, 7–15 cm long **Flowers:** deep pink (rarely white), 6 mm across, with 5 backward-pointing petals below a crown of 5 cups (hoods) each with a slender horn projecting beyond its tip; flowers borne in round, umbrella-like clusters **Blooms:** June to August **Fruits:** erect, paired, lance-shaped pods 5–10 cm long, splitting down 1 side to release flat seeds with silky parachutes **Habitat:** wet, sunny sites **Distribution:** native from Quebec to Manitoba, south through the central and eastern U.S. **Pick:** a few; caution

Bittersweet Nightshade
Solanum dulcamara

This common weed is poisonous to both humans and livestock. Unfortunately, its bright red berries often attract the attention of small children. The roots and stems are said to taste bitter at first and then sweet, hence the name *dulcamara*, 'bittersweet.' • Bittersweet nightshade was introduced to North America as a medicinal ornamental. In Europe, it was used for treating coughs, fevers and other illnesses, and it was applied to warts, pimples, swellings and aching joints. • The important nightshade family, with its distinctive, rocket-shaped flowers, includes potatoes, tomatoes and tobacco.

Plant: clambering perennial 1–3 m tall, with woody base **Leaves:** 2.5–8 cm long, heart-shaped or with 2 lobes or leaflets at the base **Flowers:** purple to pale blue, 1–1.5 cm across, with 5 backward-pointing petal lobes around a yellow 'beak' of fused anthers; flowers hanging in clusters of 10–25 **Blooms:** May to September **Fruits:** bright red berries 8–11 mm long **Habitat:** various; usually moist sites **Distribution:** Eurasia; naturalized across temperate North America **Pick:** freely; caution

Spreading Dogbane
Apocynum androsaemifolium

Danger lurks in these delicate bells. Each flower conceals five nectaries inside five V-shaped openings edged with tiny teeth. Insects, drawn to the fragrant nectar, often catch their feet in these openings and cannot escape. Fortunately, bees and butterflies are strong enough to free themselves and carry pollen to other flowers. • Women of some tribes rolled dogbane stem fibres on their legs to make fine thread, said to be finer and stronger than the best cotton thread. It was used for sewing and for making twine, nets, fabric and bowstrings. The poisonous, acrid sap was said to stimulate hair growth by irritating the follicles, but people with sensitive skin are more likely to develop blisters than hair.

Plant: erect, blue-green perennial 20–100 cm tall, usually bushy, with milky sap
Leaves: paired, 3–10 cm long, often drooping
Flowers: pinkish, bell-shaped, 6–10 mm across, with 5 spreading lobes; flowers nodding on slender stalks in branched clusters
Blooms: June to August **Fruits:** hanging, paired, slender pods, 5–15 cm long, splitting down 1 side to release seeds with silky-white parachutes **Habitat:** sunny, well drained sites
Distribution: native from Newfoundland to Alaska to southern U.S. **Pick:** freely; caution

Swamp Vervain
Verbena hastata

S wamp vervain's small, deep blue blossoms develop in a ring, starting at the bottom of the flower spike. As the ring approaches the top, the spike often produces more buds at its tip, sometimes extending the flowering period to three months. • This plant has been used for many years as a medicinal herb for treating convalescents and people suffering from depression, headaches, jaundice, cramps, coughs and fevers. Externally, it has been applied to wounds, ulcers and acne. Swamp vervain can, however, interfere with blood pressure medication and hormone therapy, and large doses cause vomiting and diarrhea.

Plant: rough-hairy perennial 40–150 cm tall, with square, grooved, branched stems **Leaves:** paired, 4–18 cm long, lance-shaped, often with 2 small lobes at the base, irregularly coarse-toothed, stalked **Flowers:** violet blue, funnel-shaped, 2.5–4.5 mm across, with 5 flaring lobes; many flowers in branched, candelabra-like clusters of stiff, compact spikes **Blooms:** July to September **Fruits:** 4 slender nutlets, 1.5–2 mm long **Habitat:** moist, open sites **Distribution:** native in southern Canada and throughout the U.S.; rare in western Canada **Pick:** a few

Common Viper's Bugloss
Echium vulgare

Common viper's bugloss was introduced to North America as a garden flower in the 1600s; by the mid-1800s, agriculturalists were condemning it as a vile foreign weed. Although it is said to be edible, it would make a rather bristly dish. In fact, some people get rashes by simply touching this hairy plant. The beautiful flowers, on the other hand, make a pretty garnish when floated in punch or tossed in salads. • At one time, common viper's bugloss was said to have the power to drive away sadness, especially when mixed with wine. It was also believed to counteract viper venom, and therefore to cure all snake bites. Unfortunately, it was most effective when administered before the bite, which required a certain amount of foresight.

Plant: rough-hairy biennial 30–80 cm tall, from taproot **Leaves:** oblong to lance-shaped, 6–25 cm long, smaller upwards **Flowers:** bright blue to violet purple (buds pink), asymmetrically funnel-shaped, 1.2–2 cm across, with 4 reddish stamens and a slender style projecting from the mouth; many flowers in elongating clusters with uncoiling, 1-sided branches **Blooms:** June to August **Fruits:** 4 small, rough nutlets **Habitat:** disturbed sites **Distribution:** Europe and north Africa; naturalized from Newfoundland to B.C., Alaska and Texas **Pick:** freely; caution

Creeping Bellflower
Campanula rapunculoides

Creeping bellflower was first brought to Canada as a hardy garden flower, but it has also been planted as a vegetable. The tender young leaves have been eaten raw or cooked as a potherb, and the fleshy roots are said to have a slightly sweet, nutty flavour when roasted or boiled. • This plant usually spreads via underground runners, but a single plant can produce as many as 3000 seeds. Once established, creeping bell-flower often spreads aggressively, choking out other species and becoming a troublesome weed. • The name *Campanula* comes from the Latin *campana*, 'bell,' in reference to the bell-like flowers. Although an old common name is 'Our Lady's thimble,' the bells were also believed to provide thimbles for witches.

Plant: erect perennial 30–100 cm tall, from spreading rootstock with fleshy vertical roots **Leaves:** coarse, irregularly toothed, 1.5–8 cm long, rounded to heart-shaped at the stem base, gradually narrower and shorter-stalked upwards **Flowers:** blue to violet, bell-shaped, 5-lobed, 2.5–3.5 cm long; flowers nodding in stiff, 1-sided, elongating clusters **Blooms:** July to August **Fruits:** round, nodding capsules, opening near the base **Habitat:** disturbed ground **Distribution:** Eurasia; naturalized across temperate North America (except Saskatchewan) **Pick:** freely

Harebell
Campanula rotundifolia

This delicate, nodding wild-flower is the famous bluebell of Scotland. Although harebell is a hardy, resilient plant, it is also the essence of fragility, with graceful blue bells bobbing on hair-like stems. Small insects find it difficult to crawl inside these flowers to steal pollen and nectar, but bees and other flying pollinators have easy access. • The nodding bells trap warm air and protect styles and stamens from rain. Mature capsules sway back and forth on slender elastic stalks, scattering seeds from holes in their sides like swinging salt shakers. • The epithet for this species, *rotundifolia*, refers to the round leaves at the base of the plant, but these leaves have usually withered away by the time the flowers open.

Plant: slender perennial 10–80 cm tall
Leaves: mainly on stem, slender, stalkless, 1.5–8 cm long; rounded, stalked basal leaves also present but soon fade
Flowers: blue, bell-shaped, 5-lobed, 1.5–2.5 cm long; 1 to many on thread-like stalks in loose, elongating clusters
Blooms: June to September
Fruits: nodding capsules, opening by pores on the sides near the base
Habitat: well-drained, often rocky sites
Distribution: native across North America south to Mexico, and around the world **Pick:** a few

Field Bindweed
Convolvulus arvensis

This small, twining plant bears charming, morning-glory-like flowers. Unfortunately, it can soon become a most troublesome weed, clambering over other plants in a smothering blanket of leaves and flowers. The name *Convolvulus* comes from the Latin *convolvere*, 'to entwine.' Tendrils wind tightly around any slender support nearby, sometimes completing a 360° twist every 100 minutes. Although each plant is capable of producing more than 500 long-lived seeds, field bindweed seldom fruits. Instead, plants usually reproduce by vegetative means. Spreading rootstocks stretch up to 4 m, sending up new shoots along the way. When broken, even small pieces of these deep, brittle runners can grow into new plants. Newly established field bindweed plants also release toxins into the soil to poison other species and reduce competition for water, nutrients and sunlight.

Plant: slender, trailing or climbing perennial, with 30–100 cm stems from deep, spreading rootstock **Leaves:** triangular to arrowhead-shaped, 2–5 cm long **Flowers:** white to pink, broadly funnel-shaped, 1.5–2.5 cm across, twisted in bud; flowers single or paired on long stalks from leaf axils
Blooms: May to September **Fruits:** small, cone-shaped capsules, usually hanging
Habitat: disturbed ground **Distribution:** Europe; naturalized across southern Canada and throughout the U.S. **Pick:** freely

Hedge False-Bindweed
Calystegia sepium

The name *Calystegia*, 'beautiful covering,' refers to the two leafy bracts that enclose the bud and later cover the base of this flower. The name could just as easily refer to this plant's lovely lush mats of triangular leaves, which are dotted with showy, white to pink flowers. Each tightly twisted flower bud unwinds into a broad funnel during the day, retwisting at night and when it has finished blooming. Pink or white lines (nectar guides) inside the funnel lead bugs to five nectar-containing holes at the bottom.
• Although hedge false-bindweed can be a serious weed, it can produce striking flowered blankets when allowed to trail over walls and fences. Several European forms have been introduced as garden plants, and today both native and introduced forms grow wild in eastern North America.

Plant: climbing or trailing perennial, with 1–3 m long stems from spreading rootstock **Leaves:** arrowhead-shaped, 5–12 cm long **Flowers:** white to pink, broadly funnel-shaped, 4–7 cm across, with 5 sepals enclosed by 2 heart-shaped, 1–2 cm bracts; flowers long-stalked, single in leaf axils **Blooms:** May to September **Fruits:** cone-shaped capsules, usually hanging **Habitat:** moist, often disturbed sites **Distribution:** native in temperate North America and Eurasia **Pick:** freely

Page numbers indicate where terms are illustrated.

achene: a small, dry fruit that doesn't split open when mature, often seed-like in appearance, distinguished from a nutlet by its relatively thin wall (p. 135)

alternate: situated singly at each joint or node (e.g., as leaves on a stem) or regularly between other organs (e.g., as stamens alternate with petals) (p. 133)

annual: a plant that completes its life cycle in one growing season

anther: the pollen-bearing part of a stamen (pp. 10, 135)

ascending: growing upwards on an angle

axil: the angle between a side organ (e.g., a leaf) and the part to which it is attached (e.g., a stem) (p. 133)

basal: located at the base or arising from it, e.g., leaves at the base of a stem

beak: a prolonged, more or less slender tip on a thicker organ such as a fruit

berry: a fruit that is fleshy throughout and usually contains several to many seeds

biennial: living for 2 years, usually producing flowers and seed in the 2nd year

bilaterally symmetrical: divisible into 2 equal parts along 1 line only (p. 16); compare 'radially symmetrical'

blade: the broad, flat part of a leaf or petal (p. 133)

bract: a specialized leaf with a flower (or sometimes a flower cluster) arising from its axil (p. 135)

bulb: a fleshy underground organ made up of overlapping, swollen scales; e.g., an onion is a bulb

Leaf Parts and Arrangements

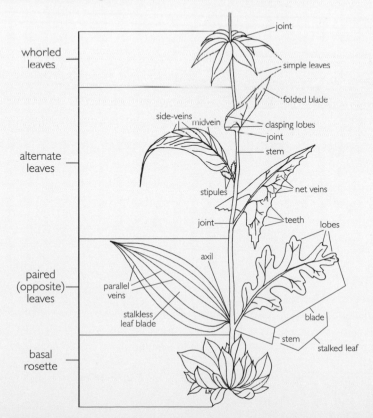

Leaf Divisions

palmately divided
(like fingers on a hand)

pinnately divided
(like barbs on a feather)

Blade Shapes

sword-like   slender
                    (linear)

oblong   lance-shaped

ovate   elliptic

oval   heart-shaped

calyx: the sepals of a flower, collectively (p. 10)

capsule: a dry fruit that splits open when mature and is capable of producing more than 1 seed

chambered: with inner cavities

channelled: with at least 1 deep lengthwise groove

circumpolar: occurring in northern regions around the world

clambering: sprawling and trailing over the ground

clasping: embracing or surrounding, usually in reference to a leaf base around a stem (p. 133)

corolla: the petals of a flower, collectively (p. 10)

creeping: growing along (or beneath) the surface of the ground and producing roots at intervals (usually at joints)

cultivar: a cultivated variety, i.e., a plant or animal originating in cultivation

drupe: a fleshy, pulpy, 1-seeded fruit in which the seed has a protective stony covering

elongating: describes a flower cluster that lengthens as it develops, with flowers and then fruits forming at the base first and then upwards to the tip; a raceme (p. 135)

family: a group of related plants or animals forming a category of biological classification above genus; e.g., the aster family (Asteraceae)

fibrous roots: slender, fibre-like roots, usually numerous and clumped

filament: the stalk of a stamen; the filament supports the anther (p. 10)

fleshy: plump, firm and pulpy; succulent

floret: a small flower, usually 1 of several in a cluster (pp. 16, 135)

flowerhead: a dense cluster of tiny flowers (florets), often appearing as a single flower; typical of the aster family (pp. 16, 135)

follicle: a dry, pod-like fruit, splitting open along a single line on 1 side

fringed: edged with a row of hairs (p. 136)

fruit: a ripened ovary, together with any other structures that ripen with it as a unit

genus [genera]: a group of related plants or animals constituting a category of biological classification below family and above species; the first word of a scientific name indicates the genus, e.g., *Achillea* in *Achillea millefolium*

gland: botanically, a surface depression, bump or appendage that produces a thick, sticky or greasy fluid

glandular: with glands

herb: a plant without woody above-ground parts, dying back to the ground in winter

introduced: brought in from another region (e.g., from Europe), not native; such exotic plants often lack predators and other population controls present in the native range

latex: milky plant juice containing rubbery compounds

leaflet: a single segment of a compound leaf (p. 134)

lip: a projection or expansion of a structure, such as the lower petal of a flower (p. 137)

lobe: a rounded or strap-shaped division of a leaf, petal or other structure (p. 133)

midvein: the central vein of a leaf (p. 133)

monoculture: a growth of only 1 kind of organism (e.g., 1 species of plant) in an area

mucilage: a sticky, gelatinous plant substance

mycorrhiza: the mutually beneficial (symbiotic) association of certain fungi with the roots of certain seed plants

native: originating in a particular place (e.g., in Ontario); indigenous

naturalized: originating in a distant region (introduced) but now adapted to the local environment and growing wild there

nerved: with prominent longitudinal lines or veins

net-veined: with a branched network of veins (p. 133)

noxious weed: an aggressive, usually introduced plant that rapidly invades sites where it is not wanted; in the legal sense, an invasive plant species requiring management or control because of legislative action

nutlet: a small, hard, dry, 1-seeded fruit or part of a fruit, not splitting open when mature

opposite: paired; situated across from each other at the same joint (not alternate or whorled) (p. 133)

ovary: the structure at the base of a pistil that contains the young, undeveloped seeds (ovules) (p. 10)

palmate: divided into 3 or more lobes or leaflets diverging from 1 point, like fingers on a hand (p. 134)

perennial: living for 3 or more years, usually flowering and fruiting for several years

persistent: remaining attached long after normal function has been completed

petal: a member of the inside ring of modified flower leaves, usually brightly colored or white (pp. 10, 135)

pinnate: with parts (branches, lobes, leaflets, veins) arranged on both sides of a central stalk or vein, like the bristles on a feather; feather-like (p. 134)

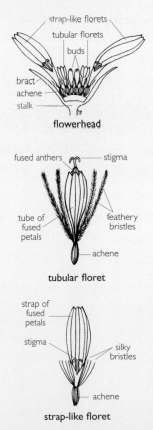

Flower Arrangements

spike   elongating cluster

leafy bracts

umbrella-shaped cluster

Parts of a Flowerhead of the Aster Family

strap-like florets

tubular florets

buds

bract

achene

stalk

flowerhead

fused anthers   stigma

tube of fused petals   feathery bristles

achene

tubular floret

strap of fused petals

stigma   silky bristles

achene

strap-like floret

Blade Edges

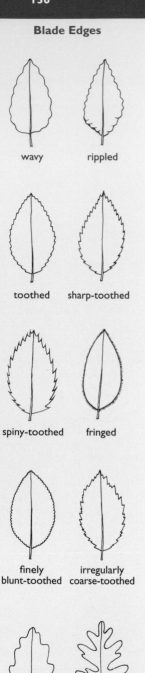

wavy   rippled

toothed   sharp-toothed

spiny-toothed   fringed

finely   irregularly
blunt-toothed coarse-toothed

shallowly   deeply
lobed   lobed

pistil: the female organ of a flower, usually consisting of an ovary, style and stigma (p. 10)

pod: a dry fruit that splits open to release its seeds

pollen: the powdery contents of an anther, each grain containing the male cells

pollinate: to transfer pollen from an anther to a stigma

pollination: the process of pollinating

prolific: producing many offspring

radially symmetrical: with parts arranged like spokes on a wheel, therefore divisible into equal parts along 2 or more lines (p. 17); compare 'bilaterally symmetrical'

rootstock: an underground, usually lengthened stem, distinguished from a true root by the presence of joints (nodes) and buds or scale-like leaves; a rhizome

rosette: a cluster of crowded, usually basal leaves in a circular arrangement (p. 133)

runner: a slender, horizontally spreading stem that often roots at its joints and tips

scale: any small, thin or flat structure

schizocarp: a dry fruit that splits into 2 or more parts when mature, e.g., fruits of the carrot family

sepal: a member of the outermost ring of modified flower leaves, usually green and more or less leafy in texture but sometimes colourful (p. 10)

sheathing: partly or wholly surrounding another organ

simple: undivided (p. 133)

species (sp.) [species, spp.]: a group of closely related plants or animals; the fundamental unit of biological classification, indicated by the second word of a scientific name (the specific epithet), e.g., *millefolium* in *Achillea millefolium*

specific epithet: see 'species'

spike: a simple, unbranched flower cluster, with (essentially) stalkless flowers arranged on an elongated main stalk (p. 135)

spreading: diverging from the vertical, approaching horizontal

spur: a hollow appendage on a petal or sepal, usually functioning as a nectary (p. 137)

stamen: the pollen-bearing (male) organ of a flower consisting of an anther and a filament (p. 10)

sterile: incapable of producing seed

stigma: the tip of the female organ (pistil), where the pollen lands (pp. 10, 135)

stipules: a pair of bract-like or leaf-like appendages at the base of a leaf stalk (p. 133)

strap-like floret: a small, often showy flower (floret) with a narrow, ribbon-like strap of fused petals, in a flowerhead of the aster family; a ray floret (p. 135)

style: the part of the pistil connecting the stigma to the ovary, often elongated and stalk-like (p. 10)

subspecies (ssp.): a group of closely related plants or animals within a species, ranked between species and variety in biological classification

taproot: a root system with a prominent main root, directed vertically downwards and bearing smaller side roots, sometimes becoming very swollen and containing stored food material (starch or sugar); e.g., a carrot is a taproot

tendril: a slender, clasping or twining outgrowth from a stem or leaf (p. 134)

tepal: a sepal or petal, when these structures are not easily distinguished

tooth: a small, often pointed lobe on the edge of a plant part (usually on a leaf) (pp. 133, 136)

trailing: spreading flat on the ground but not rooting

tuber: a thickened portion of a below-ground stem or root, serving for food storage and often also for propagation; e.g., a potato is a stem tuber

tubular floret: a small, tubular flower (floret) with fused petals, in a flowerhead of the aster family; a disc floret (p. 135)

umbrella-shaped cluster: a branched flower grouping in which the branches radiate from one joint and curve upwards like the ribs of an umbrella to produce a flat-topped to rounded cluster; an umbel (p. 135)

variety (var.): a group of similar variants of a species, ranked below subspecies in biological classification

vegetative reproduction: producing new plants from asexual parts (e.g., rootstocks, leaves, stem fragments); the offspring are genetically identical to (i.e., clones of) the parent plant

vein: a strand of conducting tubes (i.e., a vascular bundle containing phloem and xylem), especially if visible externally, as in a leaf (p. 133)

weed: a common, undesirable or troublesome plant that grows in abundance, especially on cultivated or waste ground; many of our weeds have been introduced from Eurasia

whorl: a ring of 3 or more similar structures (e.g., leaves, branches or flowers) arising from 1 joint or node (p. 133)

wing: a thin, flattened expansion on the side(s) or tip of a plant part, e.g., on a seed or a stalk

winged: with 1 or more wings

Flower Shapes

tubular   funnel-shaped

bell-shaped   cupped

saucer-shaped

cross-shaped (4-petalled)

pea-like

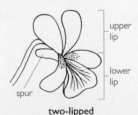

spur

upper lip

lower lip

two-lipped

Bown, D. (1995). *Encyclopedia of Herbs and Their Uses*. Montreal, RD Press.

Chambers, B., K. Legasy et al. (1996). *Forest Plants of Central Ontario*. Edmonton, Alberta, Lone Pine Publishing.

Coffey, T. (1993). *The History and Folklore of North American Wildflowers*. New York, Facts on File.

Couplan, F. (1998). *The Encyclopedia of Edible Plants of North America*. New Canaan, Connecticut, Keats Publishing.

Erichsen-Brown, C. (1979). *Use of Plants for the Past 500 Years*. Aurora, Ontario, Breezy Creeks Press.

Fernald, M.L. (1950). *Gray's Manual of Botany*. New York, American Book Company.

Foster, S. and J.A. Duke (1990). *Field Guide to Medicinal Plants: Eastern and Central North America*. Boston, Houghton Mifflin.

Gleason, H.A. and A. Cronquist (1991). *Manual of Vascular Plants of Northeastern United States and Adjacent Canada*. Bronx, The New York Botanical Garden.

Grieve, M. (1931). *A Modern Herbal*. Harmondsworth, Middlesex, England, Jonathan Cape. Republished in 1976 by Penguin Books.

Kershaw, L. (2000). *Edible and Medicinal Plants of the Rockies*. Edmonton, Alberta, Lone Pine Publishing.

Lacey, L. (1993). *Micmac Medicines: Remedies and Recollections*. Halifax, Nova Scotia, Nimbus Publishing.

Marles, R.L., C. Clavelle et al. (2000). *Aboriginal Plant Use in Canada's Northwest Boreal Forest*. Vancouver, UBC Press.

Morton, J.K. and J.M. Venn (2000). *The Flora of Manitoulin Island and Adjacent Islands in Lake Huron, Georgian Bay and the North Channel*. Waterloo, Ontario, Department of Biology, University of Waterloo.

Mulligan, G.A. and D.B. Munro (1990). *Poisonous Plants of Canada*. Ottawa, Agriculture Canada.

Newmaster, S.G., A.G. Harris et al. (1997). *Wetland Plants of Ontario*. Edmonton, Alberta, Lone Pine Publishing.

Niering, W.A. and N.C. Olmstead (1979). *National Audubon Society Field Guide to North American Wildflowers*. New York, Alfred A. Knopf.

Peirce, A. (1999). *The American Pharmaceutical Association Practical Guide to Natural Medicines*. New York, William Morrow and Company.

Peterson, L.A. (1977). *A Field Guide to Edible Wild Plants of Eastern and Central North America*. Boston, Houghton Mifflin.

Peterson, R.T. and M. McKenny (1968). *Northeastern Wildflowers: A Field Guide to Wildflowers*. New York, Houghton Mifflin.

Pond, B. (1974). *A Sampler of Wayside Herbs: Discovering Old Uses for Familiar Wild Plants*. Riverside, Connecticut, Chatham Press.

Reader's Digest (1986). *Magic and Medicine of Plants*. Montreal, The Reader's Digest Association.

Royer, F. and R. Dickinson (1998). *Weeds of Canada and the Northern United States: A Guide for Identification*. Edmonton, Alberta, University of Alberta Press.

Stokes, D. and L. Stokes (1985). *A Guide to Enjoying Wildflowers*. Toronto, Little, Brown.

Szczawinski, A.F. and N.J. Turner (1980). *Wild Green Vegetables of Canada*. Ottawa, National Museum of Natural Sciences, National Museums of Canada.

Szczawinski, A.F. and N.J. Turner (1988). *Edible Garden Weeds of Canada*. Ottawa, National Museum of Natural Sciences, National Museums of Canada.

Turner, N.J. and A.F. Szczawinski (1978). *Wild Coffee and Tea Substitutes of Canada*. Ottawa, National Museum of Natural Sciences, National Museums of Canada.

Westbrooks, R.G. and J.W. Preacher (1986). *Poisonous Plants of Eastern North America*. Columbia, South Carolina, University of South Carolina Press.

White, D.J., E. Haber et al. (1993). *Invasive Plants of Natural Habitats in Canada*. Ottawa, Canadian Wildlife Service, Environment Canada, Canadian Museum of Nature.

Two-Sided Flowers

- yellow lady's-slipper
- pink corydalis
- butter-and-eggs
- wild bergamot
- selfheal
- catnip
- spotted touch-me-not
- early blue violet
- beach pea
- perennial sweet pea
- bird vetch
- bigleaf lupine
- purple crown-vetch
- bird's-foot trefoil
- sweet-clover
- alfalfa

Tiny Stalkless Flowers in Compact Clusters

- rabbitfoot clover
- alsike clover
- red clover
- English plantain
- common teasel
- lesser burdock
- Canada thistle
- bull thistle
- nodding plumeless-thistle
- spotted knapweed
- brown knapweed
- chicory
- tall blue lettuce
- prickly lettuce
- hairy cat's-ear
- yellow hawkweed
- orange hawkweed
- perennial sow-thistle
- common dandelion
- common goat's-beard

- annual sunflower
- elecampane
- black-eyed Susan
- oxeye daisy
- scentless chamomile
- pineapple-weed
- common tansy
- Canada goldenrod
- common yarrow
- pearly everlasting
- fringed aster
- Philadelphia fleabane
- spotted Joe-Pye weed

Tiny Stalked Flowers in Branched Clusters

- leafy spurge
- Queen Anne's lace
- wild parsnip
- common cow-parsnip
- common water-parsnip
- spotted water-hemlock
- northern bedstraw
- hoary alyssum
- curly dock
- tall meadowrue

Circular Flowers with Distinct Petals

- pickerelweed
- buckbean
- wapato
- starry false Solomon's-seal
- white death-camas
- snow trillium
- wood lily
- orange daylily
- northern blue flag
- common blue-eyed-grass

- white water-lily
- yellow pond-lily
- yellow marsh-marigold
- meadow buttercup
- Canada anemone
- wild mustard
- tumbleweed mustard
- sulphur cinquefoil
- common silverweed
- Virginia strawberry
- bunchberry
- cultivated flax
- musk mallow
- bouncing Bet
- bladder campion
- common St. John's-wort
- purple loosestrife
- common fireweed
- hairy willowherb
- common evening-primrose
- great mullein
- fringed yellow-loosestrife
- common milkweed
- swamp milkweed
- bittersweet nightshade

Circular Flowers with Fused Petals

- spreading dogbane
- swamp vervain
- common viper's bugloss
- creeping bellflower
- harebell
- field bindweed
- hedge false-bindweed

Common Name	Scientific Name	Page Numbers
Aster Family	Asteraceae	53–80
Bellflower Family	Campanulaceae	129–130
Borage Family	Boraginaceae	128
Buckbean Family	Menyanthaceae	92
Buckwheat Family	Polygonaceae	89
Buttercup Family	Ranunculaceae	90, 103–105
Carrot Family	Apiaceae	82–86
Dogbane Family	Apocynaceae	126
Dogwood Family	Cornaceae	111
Evening-primrose Family	Onagraceae	118–120
Figwort Family	Scrophulariaceae	34, 121
Flax Family	Linaceae	112
Fumitory Family	Fumiariaceae	33
Iris Family	Iridaceae	99–100
Lily Family	Liliaceae	94–98
Loosestrife Family	Lythraceae	117
Madder Family	Rubiaceae	87
Mallow Family	Malvaceae	113
Milkweed Family	Asclepiadaceae	123–124
Mint Family	Lamiaceae	35–37
Morning-glory Family	Convolvulaceae	131–132
Mustard Family	Brassicaceae	88, 106–107
Nightshade Family	Solanaceae	125
Orchid Family	Orchidaceae	32
Pea Family	Fabaceae	40–50
Pickerelweed Family	Pontederiaceae	91
Pink Family	Caryophyllaceae	114–115
Plantain Family	Plantaginaceae	51
Primrose Family	Primulaceae	122
Rose Family	Rosaceae	108–110
Spurge Family	Euphorbiaceae	81
St. John's-wort Family	Clusiaceae	116
Teasel Family	Dipsacaceae	52
Touch-me-not Family	Balsaminaceae	38
Vervain Family	Verbenaceae	127
Violet Family	Violaceae	39
Water-lily Family	Nymphaeaceae	101–102
Water-plantain Family	Alismataceae	93

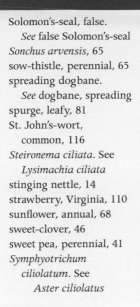

Photo: Jen Lusk

*A*n avid naturalist since her childhood in Ontario, Linda Kershaw focused on botany at the University of Waterloo, earning her master's degree in 1976. Since then she has worked as a consultant and researcher in northwestern Canada and as an author and editor in Edmonton, while pursuing two favourite pastimes: photography and illustrating. Linda is the author or co-author of seven Lone Pine field guides, including the recent *Trees of Ontario*.

Over many years in the field with Linda, sons Geoff (left, 15 field seasons) and Eric (20 seasons) and husband Peter (far right, 28 seasons) have travelled thousands of kilometres and developed sharp eyes in the never-ending search for wild plants and animals. They've also learned the virtue of patience as 15-minute walks turn into two-hour photo sessions. Linda dedicates this book to her family, to thank them for their continued patience and support and for many happy hours of hiking through wild and not-so-wild places.